FORTHCOMING TITLES

Occupational Therapy for the Brain-Injured Adult
Jo Clark-Wilson and Gordon Muir Giles

Multiple Sclerosis
Approaches to management
Lorraine De Souza

Physiotherapy in Respiratory and Intensive Care
Alexandra Hough

Understanding Dysphasia
Lesley Jordan and Rita Twiston Davies

Management in Occupational Therapy
Zielfa B. Maslin

Speech and Language Problems in Children
Dilys A. Treharne

THERAPY IN PRACTICE SERIES
Edited by Jo Campling

This series of books is aimed at 'therapists' concerned with rehabilitation in a very broad sense. The intended audience particularly includes occupational therapists, physiotherapists and speech therapists, but many titles will also be of interest to nurses, psychologists, medical staff, social workers, teachers or volunteer workers. Some volumes are interdisciplinary, others are aimed at one particular profession. All titles will be comprehensive but concise, and practical but with due reference to relevant theory and evidence. They are not research monographs but focus on professional practice, and will be of value to both students and qualified personnel.

Autism

Professional perspectives and practice

Edited by KATHRYN ELLIS
Family Services Coordinator
The National Autistic Society

Published in association with
the National Autistic Society

CHAPMAN AND HALL

LONDON • NEW YORK • TOKYO • MELBOURNE • MADRAS

UK	Chapman and Hall, 11 New Fetter Lane, London EC4P 4EE
USA	Chapman and Hall, 29 West 35th Street, New York NY10001
JAPAN	Chapman and Hall Japan, Thomson Publishing Japan, Hirakawacho Nemoto Building, 7F, 1-7-11 Hirakawa-cho, Chiyoda-ku, Tokyo 102
AUSTRALIA	Chapman and Hall Australia, Thomas Nelson Australia, 480 La Trobe Street, PO Box 4725, Melbourne 3000
INDIA	Chapman and Hall India, R. Sheshadri, 32 Second Main Road, CIT East, Madras 600 035

First edition 1990

© 1990 Kathryn Ellis

Typeset in 10/12pt Times by Mayhew Typesetting, Bristol
Printed in Great Britain by St Edmundsbury Press Ltd,
Bury St Edmunds, Suffolk

ISBN 0 412 32220 X

British Library Cataloguing in Publication Data

Autism.
1. Man. Autism
I. Ellis, Kathryn II. National Austistic Society
III. Series
616.8982

ISBN 0 412 32220 X

Dedicated to the life of Derek Ricks
BA, MD, FRCPsych, DPM (1928–1988)

Staunch advocate and generous friend to
people with autism and their families

Contents

Contributors

Wendy Brown
Principal
Broomhayes School
Devon

Alison Elliot
Principal
The Queen Elizabeth Queen Mother Centre
Hertfordshire

Rita Jordan
Senior Lecturer in Special Education
Hatfield Polytechnic

William Meldrum
Director of Development
Scottish Society for Autistic Children

Gillian Taylor
Former Principal
The Helen Allison School
Kent

Lorna Wing
Honorary Senior Lecturer
Institute of Psychiatry

Foreword

When I took up post as Director of the National Autistic Society in May 1989, this book was nearing completion. One of my first tasks was to read and approve the manuscript. What a pleasure that was – coming new to the field of autism but with a professional background in social work, training and research, I found it a book which really put me in touch with a condition which is little understood and often not recognized or diagnosed outside specialist circles.

This book is written by experienced practitioners who have worked closely with children and adults with autism and who use their direct involvement in their education and care to relate theory to practice. The introductory chapter by Lorna Wing lays out clearly what is known about the causation and consequences of autism, and views it in the context of other developmental disorders. The rest of the chapter takes different stages of development, from infancy to adulthood, and examines the rationale underlying particular teaching, care and management approaches.

Because there are so few specialist resources for children and people with autism, the number of practitioners with in-depth knowledge and first-hand experience of the condition are few and far between. In this book a wealth of such experience is sensitively drawn together and illustrated with case histories; consequently carers, professionals new to working with people with autism and those who want to improve their specialist skills in the field, will all find something practical, and useful to encourage them in their tasks.

At a time when service provision for all client groups is undergoing radical changes in the light of such developments as the introduction of the National Curriculum, the reform of the National Health Service and the implications for Social Services Departments of the Griffiths Report, this book provides some clear examples of the special needs of children and adults with autism, which can help professionals to develop appropriate services within the new frameworks.

The selection of approaches in this book builds on the work of the National Autistic Society, families and professionals, to provide relevant effective care for people with autism. The result is a book which should enable people to obtain a wealth of information, both about the needs of the client group and the carers who work with them. It fills a much needed gap in identifying the strengths and pitfalls of different approaches and is a welcome asset in a field where all too little is known.

The National Autistic Society is always looking for new ways to give help and encouragement to those who provide any kind of care for children and adults who are autistic. Here we have a book which has something to offer to many different groups and I am sure it will become essential reading for all with an interest in autism.

Geraldine Peacock
Executive Director
The National Autistic Society

1

What is autism?

Lorna Wing

'Please explain, in just a few words, exactly what is autism'. This request, made by journalists or radio or television interviewers, inevitably produces a sinking of the heart in the hapless informant. Autism is the name given to a behaviour pattern, produced in a complicated way, as the end result of a long chain of causation and there is no way of explaining it in a few words. But, given the luxury of a whole chapter devoted to the task, justice can be done to the strange story of the nature and causes of autism and how it fits into the wide range of disorders of development of psychological functions.

HISTORICAL PERSPECTIVE

In 1943, Leo Kanner, a child psychiatrist in the USA, described 11 children who had in common a peculiar pattern of behaviour. This pattern comprised many different features but Kanner thought the main ones to be as follows: a profound lack of emotional contact with other people; absence of speech or else peculiar, idiosyncratic ways of speaking that do not seem designed for conversation; fascination with objects and skill in manipulating them; an anxiously obsessive desire for preserving sameness in the environment and/or familiar routines; evidence for potentially good intelligence shown by facial appearance and feats of memory, or skill in performance tasks involving fitting and assembly tasks, such as inset and jig-saw puzzles. Kanner considered that these features defined a specific syndrome that was quite different from all other childhood conditions, and decided to name it 'early infantile autism'. (The term autism had, before this, been used to describe the social withdrawal

1

found in adult schizophrenia, and this led to confusion of the two conditions which has, to varying degrees, affected attitudes ever since.)

Although Kanner was the first person to perceive that a group of children shared a particular behaviour pattern, descriptions of individual children with similar problems can be found in the historical literature. Perhaps the legends of 'changeling children', strong, difficult, demanding little creatures left in place of real human children stolen by the fairies, were based on observations of children with autism. The French physician, Itard, wrote detailed descriptions of the behaviour of Victor, the 12 year old boy placed in his charge who, in the late 18th century, had been found wandering wild in the woods of Aveyron. No parent can read Itard's reports without becoming convinced by all the telling details that Victor was autistic.

At the end of the 19th and during the early years of the 20th century, a number of psychiatrists described children with various forms of abnormal behaviour who were generally referred to as 'psychotic', but at least some of whom were probably autistic in Kanner's sense of the term. In 1942, just one year before Kanner's first paper on the subject, the famous psychologists, Gesell and Amatreeda, in a textbook on child development, included a brief account of children who were impaired in social interaction and communication, repetitive in behaviour, with some isolated patchy abilities, especially in visuo-spatial skills, and who tended to look normal in appearance. This group were clearly closely similar to those described by Kanner. Both Kanner on the one hand and Gesell and Amatreeda on the other, recognized that these children had in common a peculiar behaviour pattern but, while Kanner believed the children to be of potentially normal, even superior intelligence, Gesell and Amatreeda considered that most had intelligence quotients below 50, that is in the range of the most severe learning disorders.

One year after Kanner's original paper, an Austrian psychiatrist, Hans Asperger, wrote about a group of adolescents who were odd in their social relationships and lacked empathy with others, had very poor non-verbal communication and speech that was grammatical but long-winded, literal in content and abnormal in intonation, engaged in repetitive activities, disliked change in routine and were absorbed in special interests such as railway time-tables or the movement of the planets. They had good rote memories, but poor grasp of abstract ideas. They tended to have some odd bodily movements and many were clumsy and ill-coordinated in complex movements. He referred to this cluster of features as 'autistic psychopathy'.

Yet further complication has been introduced by authors who have described children with motor clumsiness, repetitive speech and marked abnormalities of social interaction and referred to them as having 'central processing difficulties'. Also, linguists have published accounts of children with repetitive speech and severe problems with 'social-interpersonal aspects and verbal behaviour' which they have called 'pragmatic disorders'. And, in the field of psychiatry, the term 'schizoid personality' has been used for young adults, many of whom closely resemble those described by Asperger.

Most of the workers referred to above believed, like Kanner, that they were talking about separate conditions. They either did not mention, or else dismissed the possibility that all of these 'syndromes' overlapped with each other. But, to the unbiased reader, the many similarities are striking. In particular, all the writers emphasized the peculiar nature and impairment of social interaction in the children concerned.

PARENTS' PERSPECTIVE

Another facet of the problem of definition began to become apparent in the 1960s. Throughout history there have been parents who have struggled to provide the best help they could for their handicapped children but it was not until this century that associations of parents began to be formed. The voluntary body concerned with children who are autistic was formed in 1962. One of its first major objectives was the establishment of schools specializing in teaching children with autism.

The success of these efforts to draw attention to the special needs of such children and to develop specific teaching techniques highlighted the practical as well as the theoretical problems of defining the boundaries of the autistic condition. Many children with classic autism were referred for specialized education but so were
who had some though not all of the typic
to benefit from the same methods of teac
with autistic behaviour, individual children
of performance on intelligence tests could l
even more difficult, it began to be apparei
could occur in association with all kinds of
deafness, blindness, cerebral palsy, epilepsy
Down's syndrome. How was it possible to
apparently conflicting information?

4

AN EPIDEMIOLOGICAL STUDY

One way of helping to solve the problem was to move outside the clinics and schools, because the children seen in those environments had been selected for referral. An examination of all the children in one defined geographical area (an epidemiological study) would remove the problem of a referral bias. It would show whether there really were clear-cut boundaries between the various conditions described in the literature and would clarify the relationship between autism and level of intellectual ability. The present author together with colleagues in the Medical Research Council Social Psychiatry Unit carried out such a study in the former London Borough of Camberwell.

From among the children whose parents lived in Camberwell on 31st December 1970, we identified and examined in detail all those aged under 15 years on that day who had either severe or profound learning disorders or some features of autistic behaviour (however mild or doubtful) or both of these problems together. Altogether there were 173 children but five died and one was lost to the study before the initial examination. Those still alive were followed up 12–15 years later when they were all aged 16 years or over.

There were many interesting findings but those relevant to the present discussion are set out below.

Sociability and social impairment

First, the total group of 167 children seen could be divided into two sub-groups. As would be expected, some children were on the borderline and hard decisions had to be made but, in most cases, individuals could be clearly placed in one or other of the two categories.

There were 72 whose social interaction was normal in the light of their mental age, including 14 who were non-mobile. They were interested in other human beings, responded to approaches and were able to take turns in social interchanges. Even if they had no speech, they used whatever other methods were available such as gesture, facial expression or eye pointing to communicate. The other 95 children, including 16 who could not walk, were impaired in the development of their social interaction skills, even having regard to overall level of development. This type of impairment was different from the social problems found in children who are deprived, or conduct disordered.

The quality of the social impairment varied in form. Some children were aloof and indifferent to other people, especially other children. They related to adults only as mechanical providers of simple needs such as food, and tended to move away if attempts were made to communicate. Some children passively accepted approaches from other people, including children, but never made contacts spontaneously or showed any positive desire for social interaction. Others did make approaches to others, mainly adults, but in a peculiar one-sided, repetitive fashion. Their main aim appeared to be to ask endless questions over and over again, or to talk about one subject, such as aeroplanes, without regard to the interests of the listener.

It might seem that these different forms of social impairment had no relation to each other. However, there was no clear borderline between the different types and they formed a continuum rather than discrete entities. Furthermore, the follow-up showed that, over the course of development, a child could move from one form of social interaction to another.

Communication and imagination

The second relevant finding from the study was that social impairment, in any of the above forms, was closely associated with certain other problems, namely impairment of the development of social communication and social imagination together with a marked tendency to a rigid, stereotyped, repetitive pattern of activities in place of the usual imaginative, pretend play.

Each of these problems could occur in different forms. Impairment of the development of social communic   ried from total absence of understanding, or use of, any form the presence of all the mechanics of co tion, perfect grammar, wide vocabulai these for normal interchange of idea aspects of communication, such as g intonation, loudness and softness of be abnormal in some way. (Avoi mentioned as a feature of autism. appropriate use of eye contact which long and too hard, as well as avoi

Impairments of imaginative deve absence of any pretend play throug familiar situations from real life or the television, performed either with toys or by the children themselves. In all cases the major problem was poverty of *social* imagination and empathy – a difficulty in recognizing that other people had thoughts and feelings.

Rigid, repetitive behaviour was as variable as all the other impairments. The simplest form was bodily directed such as rocking, teeth-grinding or finger-flicking. Then there were children who had complex whole body movements, or whose repetitive behaviour was concerned with the collection or arrangements of objects. Others insisted on particular daily routines being followed to the last detail. Yet others showed their rigidity in repetitive speech or in the special, circumscribed interests described by Asperger.

Levels of ability

The third relevant finding from the study was that the cluster of impairments described above could be seen in children of all levels of intelligence, and in association with any other type of developmental delay or abnormality. In most cases, the profile on intelligence testing was markedly uneven, with non-verbal visuospatial skills being better than those requiring understanding or use of language. In the minority who had apparently better language-based skills, these were due to a good rote memory for words and facts, not to a real grasp of abstract ideas. A very few children had isolated high-level skills, in music, drawing or ability to calculate dates, in contrast to the rest of their performance. Most responded with pleasure to music in contrast to the lack of interest in speech.

In general, the lower the level of overall intelligence, the more likely was the child to be socially aloof and indifferent, to have no language and to have simple, bodily directed repetitive activities. The proportions in different IQ groups are given in Table 1.1. The table also demonstrates that most children have moderate or severe learning disorders as well as social impairment. The group with classic autism overlapped with but tended to have rather higher ents than the rest of the children with social impairment.

Sub-grouping

t finding concerned the identification of the cribed by different authors. We found that it

Table 1.1 Children with social impairment*. Visuo-spatial intelligence levels (aged under 15 years)

Visuo-spatial IQ	Classically autistic (No.)	%	Other socially impaired (No.)	%	Total (No.)	%
0–49	(7)	41	(41)	66	(48)	61
50–69	(4)	24	(16)	26	(20)	25
70 +	(6)	35	(5)	8	(11)	14
Total	(17)	100	(62)	100	(79)	100

* Excluding children who are non-mobile.

was possible to find some children, among the whole range of those who were socially impaired, who fitted Kanner's classic descriptions. We also found some whom Asperger would have said had his syndrome. In fact, it was possible to find one or more example of most of the groups mentioned in the earlier part of this chapter. The trouble was that there were no sharp boundaries between one group and another and, even more important, in many cases the same child or children could be fitted into more than one group. In particular, a few children of borderline or normal intelligence levels who had the characteristics of Kanner's syndrome in early childhood changed as they grew up so that, in early adult life, their behaviour was identical to that described by Asperger.

Although the socially impaired children showed such a wide range of intellectual and practical ability, and varied so much in the manifestations of their social and related problems, they all responded best to the kind of organized, structured environment, education and management that will be described in later chapters. The eventual outcome in adult life was closely related to the level of tested intelligence in childhood, those with the highest ability doing best (see later).

Conclusions from the study

The most appropriate formulation of the findings of this and other, similar studies is that social impairment is a disorder of development and that the different manifestations, whether or not they are named as syndromes, are all part of a spectrum of related disorders, to be referred to here as the 'autistic continuum'. The whole range is more or less equivalent to the general category of 'Pervasive Developmental Disorder', used in the American Psychiatric Association's

Diagnostic and Statistical Manual, 3rd Edition, Revised (DSM-III-R), or the World Health Organisation's *International Classification of Diseases*, 10th Revision (ICD 10).

It is possible to find typical examples of various sub-groups named by authors in the field, the best known being Kanner's classic autism, but the lack of definite boundaries always causes problems when trying to categorize the difficulties experienced by any individual child. In any case, from the point of view of prescribing education and other services, it is much more important to note that the child is socially impaired and to give details of his or her skills and impairment in all areas of function than it is to say whether he or she is or is not classically autistic.

The aims of education have to vary depending on each child's potential. What one can do to help a child who is severely socially and intellectually impaired and who cannot walk independently is very different from what can be achieved with a child who is socially impaired, but of normal intelligence. Nevertheless, the methods employed all differ in important ways from those appropriate for normally sociable children of any level of ability, the underlying principles of which will be described in later chapters.

OTHER FEATURES OF AUTISTIC BEHAVIOUR

The impairments of social interaction, social communication and imagination and the rigid, repetitive behaviour are the central core of the autistic spectrum, but a number of other features are commonly found as well.

Language problems

Although the mechanics of language (grammar, vocabulary, pronunciation) may be normal in a few people in the autistic continuum, in most cases there are abnormalities. In many, language understanding and use do not develop at all. In those who do speak, there can be immature grammar, immediate and delayed echolalia with reversal of pronouns, and peculiar, idiosyncratic ways of using words. In all cases, the comprehension and use of language within a social context, rather than the understanding of its literal meaning, are impaired, however good the mechanical language skills. Delay in developing language is very common indeed.

Motor co-ordination

There can be any mixture of skills and impairment affecting motor co-ordination in children with social impairment. Some are late in walking, and clumsy and awkward in large movements. Others are agile in running and climbing. Fine finger dexterity is equally variable and skill in this area cannot be predicted from that seen in large movements. Unusual postures of the hands, with fingers hyper-extended are common. Arm flapping, jumping and tip-toe walking are frequently seen and are evidence of immaturity of development of the motor system.

By adolescence, even the children who were most agile as children have developed oddities of gait and posture, such as walking with head bowed and without swinging the arms.

Responses to sensory stimuli

Children with social impairment may respond with indifference, fascination or distress to any kind of sensory stimulation. A child may ignore some sounds, be over-sensitive to others, be indifferent to heat, cold and pain, be fascinated by shiny objects and things that spin, dislike a gentle touch but thoroughly enjoy a rough and tumble game. These abnormalities are most common in younger children and in those who are severely handicapped.

Eating, drinking and sleeping

These functions may be disturbed in children who are socially impaired. They may take the form of refusal to eat at all, bizarre restriction of diet to a few items only, or, at the other extreme, eating prodigious quantities or drinking excessive amounts of fluid.

Some children sleep very little and some keep their parents awake by screaming for hours at night. Others sleep well, and for longer hours than children of the same age who are developing normally.

Challenging behaviour

A minority of children in the autistic continuum are quiet and amenable, but most present some kind of challenging behaviour. This occurs for four main reasons.

First, the lack of competence in social interaction means that children fail to learn social rules. They go where they want, take what they want, and do what they want regardless of the situation. This can be overlooked in a toddler but causes consternation when a 10 year old pulls tins from the bottom of the pile in a supermarket, or a 15 year old strips and urinates in public.

The second reason for challenging behaviour is a response to attempts to interfere with repetitive activities or routines. This can result in temper tantrums, aggression to others, or self-injury, screaming, destructiveness, running away and so on.

The third reason is behaviour induced by panic in situations the child finds confusing and threatening. The responses can be the same as for interference with routine.

Finally, repetitive, stereotyped activities can themselves be challenging or worrying to parents or care staff. Problems can include stereotyped self-injury such as constant head banging or eye-poking, taking objects from shops or other people's houses to add to collections, making repetitive, loud, irritating noises, and many others.

THE NATURE OF SOCIAL IMPAIRMENT

Having given evidence for placing Kanner's early infantile autism within the wider autistic spectrum, the next task is to define the nature of social impairment.

The best way to do this is to consider normal development from infancy to adulthood. In order eventually to become fully functioning, independent adults, babies have to develop a wide range of abilities which are pre-programmed in their brain and bodies and which unfold in a fairly predictable sequence as they grow older. These include the obvious skills such as chewing food, talking, walking, controlling the bowel and bladder, visuo-spatial competence, and later, self care, reading, writing, number work and so on. It is only comparatively recently that workers in child development have become aware that the ability to engage in reciprocal social interaction is as much a pre-programmed skill as all the other more obvious psychological and physical functions. Of course, for their proper development, children must have at least the minimum necessary input from the environment, such as food, space to move, contact with other humans, and so on but the appropriate pre-programming within the child is absolutely essential.

Social interaction skills appear in early infancy. They include the recognition that human beings are the most significant and interesting features of the environment, the capacity to give signals that attract the attention of mothers and other carers, the ability to respond to signals from others, the positive desire to communicate and receive communications from others and, later, the development of empathy – that is awareness of, interest in, and responsiveness to other people's thoughts, feelings and ideas. It is these skills which, as has already been emphasized, are missing or impaired in children in the autistic continuum.

This problem can, rarely, occur on its own in which case the result is a child who is socially impaired but has all other skills intact. Much more often it occurs in association with impairments of other cognitive skills producing all kinds of mixtures of skills and handicaps and in all degrees of severity. When the pattern comprises severe social impairment, plus poor language but good visuo-spatial and rote memory skills then the child is likely to fit the descriptions of Kanner's syndrome. Other patterns may fit other syndromes, but many do not fit any named clinical picture. This is why it makes more sense to describe each child's profile and level of ability rather than arguing about which sub-group the child should be put into within the autistic continuum.

Underlying dysfunctions

Some workers are currently attempting to analyse the specific dysfunctions that possibly underlie the social impairments characterizing the autistic continuum. Over the years there have been various suggestions as to the reasons why children who are autistic appear to be cut off from normal social interaction. The main hypotheses were abnormalities of perception of sensory stimuli, or problems in the reception and central processing of language. Both of these problems are very commonly associated with social impairment, but they are not universal. Also, they can occur in individuals who are not socially impaired, so that they do not of themselves account for social impairment.

Some authors suggest that social interaction skills are, so to speak, programmed into the brain in humans (and other social species) as a complete package that cannot be analysed into more simple underlying components. Others believe that specific cognitive skills will be found to account for the more complex social function. For example, a group of workers hypothesizes that normal children, around 2–3 years old, develop a theory that other people have minds, and that this does not happen in socially impaired children. The problem here is that social impairment can often be observed from much earlier in life than the age at which the theory of mind develops.

Another interesting possiblity is that babies developing normally are innately capable of recognizing general categories (for example the quality of human-ness) and that recognition of specific people or objects within the general categories comes later. Perhaps autistic and other socially impaired children lack the generalized concepts and, from the start, regard each object or event in the environment as separate and unrelated to anything else. Some evidence for this can be found in studies which show that children with classic autism find great difficulty in fitting individual items of any kind into a wider meaningful context. This would have especially severe effects on the development of social understanding because this is one of the most complex aspects of human behaviour, requiring the capacity to adapt one's reactions to the demands of each different social situation.

Much of the experimental work has been carried out with children with classic autism. Its relevance to the wider group of socially impaired children needs to be examined. Another problem is how to relate ideas about social impairment to all the other commonly associated (although not universal) features described above. To be acceptable any theory of social impairment must provide answers to these questions.

BIOLOGICAL CAUSES OF SOCIAL IMPAIRMENT

The idea that autism is caused by abnormal parents using abnormal methods of child-rearing has long been abandoned by most workers in the field. Careful studies have shown that parents come from any social class and their personalities vary as much as those of the rest of the population. Despite the somewhat raised chances of having a second affected child, most have other children who develop normally and are deeply concerned about and attached to their child who is handicapped.

It is now well established that a wide variety of conditions likely to cause brain damage can be found in the histories of about half of all children in the autistic continuum. These include maternal rubella, untreated phenylketonuria, tuberose sclerosis, a form of epilepsy known as infantile spasms, anoxia at birth, virus encephalitis, and trauma of the brain. There is also good evidence from twin studies for a genetic trait associated with autism in at least some cases, and the recently discovered Fragile X chromosomal abnormality may be involved in some children.

It therefore seems very probable that, for social impairment to occur, some area or function of the brain must be involved in some way. It is rare to find any evidence of gross brain damage on examination, so the problems must lie in more subtle abnormalities of cell function or arrangement. The newer methods of brain imaging offer hope that the pathology may be identified eventually. It is likely that the main problems will be found in areas of the brain which are comparatively old in evolutionary terms, since appropriate social interaction skills are present in other social animals as well as human beings. Some interesting findings have already been made, but much more work still needs to be done.

The theory of brain dysfunction underlying social impairment fits well with the clinical findings of many different patterns of skills and handicaps in different individuals. The details of the clinical picture must depend upon which parts or functions of the brain are affected by the pathological process, and very many variations can occur. So far it has not been possible to show that any particular cause is likely to lead to any particular named syndrome. It may well be that there are meaningful sub-groups within the autistic continuum. Perhaps Kanner's syndrome is one of these. The validation of any system of sub-grouping must wait upon more precise knowledge of the neuropathology.

When discussing causes it is relevant to emphasize that, among the most intellectually able group, social impairment shades into the eccentric end of the normal continuum. It is reasonable to suggest that some people have rather poor social skills and concentrate their energies upon one or two special interests, not because of any specific brain pathology, but because of their particular mixture of personality traits. Asperger himself noted that his syndrome represented 'the extreme end of the masculine character', a good subject for a hot debate in mixed company!

CONDITIONS THAT CAN BE CONFUSED WITH THE AUTISTIC CONTINUUM

There are a number of conditions which have a superficial resemblance to the disorders in the autistic continuum.

13

Schizophrenia occurring in childhood

Autistic conditions have been called 'childhood schizophrenia' leading to much confusion. It is now clear from careful studies that the autistic continuum can be differentiated from typical schizophrenia. The former almost always begins in early childhood while the latter is rarely seen before seven years of age and becomes more common towards adolescence. The symptoms of schizophrenia include hallucinations, delusions, and abnormal experiences of external interference with one's thought and will. Problems in diagnosis arise because social impairment can look superficially like the social withdrawal of schizophrenia. Also, some socially impaired children repeat things they have heard out loud and laugh for no obvious reason. This may be interpreted, wrongly, as responding to hallucinations. Repeated acting out of characters from television, such as a robot or Batman may be thought to be delusional, whereas it is really repetitive pseudo-pretend play. Schizophrenia is extremely rare before adolescence, whilst the autistic continuum is, in comparison, more common.

Developmental language disorders

The language problems in the developmental language disorders show many similarities to those seen in socially impaired children. The differences lie in the sociability, imaginative development and desire to communicate, by any means, to compensate for the special problems seen in the purely language-disordered child. The two types of conditions overlap to some extent and there are some children on the borderline in whom the diagnosis may be difficult.

Impairment of vision and hearing

These conditions affect the development of language and communication but, as with the specific language disorders, the differentiation from social impairment rests on the social and imaginative behaviour and desire to communicate, especially when appropriate alternative methods of communication have been introduced.

Psycho-social deprivation

Growing up in conditions of social and language deprivation adversely affects social behaviour and speech development. However, the pattern of behaviour of the autistic continuum does not occur. In any case, deprived children tend to improve over a few months when moved to more stimulating environments, which is not the case with socially impaired children.

Phases of early normal development

Apart from the lack of ability to engage in reciprocal social inter-action, every aspect of autistic behaviour can be seen in babies or young children developing normally. Mothers of first babies who previously worked with autistic children are often alarmed by notic-ing, for instance, hand-flapping, fascination with lights, spinning wheels of toy cars, echolalia, and repetitive routines in their own child. The difference is that these are brief phases in normal development but last for years in a socially impaired child. This underlines the validity of the modern concept of the autistic continuum as a developmental disorder.

THE PREVALENCE OF THE PROBLEM

At least three studies in Western countries, including the one in Camberwell, have shown that autism as defined by Leo Kanner occurs in four to five in every 10 000 children. In Camberwell, an additional 16 children in 10 000 were found to be socially impaired though not classically autistic, making a total of 21 in 10 000 in the autistic continuum. There is, however, evidence that children of first generation immigrants from developing countries have a somewhat higher chance of being socially impaired, perhaps because both mother and infant are exposed to viruses, peculiar to the host coun-try, to which they have not developed any immunity. The Camber-well figures may then be on the high side, a possibility given weight by a similar study in Salford, where there was a very small immigrant population which gave a total prevalence of social impair-ment of 15 per 10 000 children.

Sex ratio

All studies have shown an excess of boys over girls, usually well over twice as many. Recent work suggests that the greater excess of boys, even as high as nine or ten or more to one girl, occurs among the children with the highest levels of ability. The excess becomes less marked the more severe the intellectual handicaps. In Camberwell, in the profoundly retarded group, the numbers of each sex were almost equal. Perhaps it takes a more severe degree of pathology to make a girl socially impaired than is the case with a boy (which perhaps justifies Asperger's remark, quoted above, about the male character!).

Asperger's syndrome

No work has been carried out as yet to examine the numbers of those with the features described by Asperger. The methods used in the Camberwell study could easily have missed those with high levels of intelligence. A study of this aspect of social impairment would be of considerable interest.

The parents

The finding of a possible genetic trait brings up the question of inheritance from parents. Although studies of parents of children who are autistic have found no particular traits of personality or child-rearing behaviour, there is some suggestion that those in the group described by Asperger are rather likely to have fathers with similar characteristics. This requires further investigation, especially since we have no idea how many men in the general population have such traits.

Age of onset

Another aspect of prevalence is the age of onset. In the vast majority of cases, social impairment of the kind described here is apparent from birth or before three years of age. Some children appear to have a period of normal development before becoming socially impaired but it is not always clear if this is really the case or due to the parents' failure to recognize the problem early on. A very few develop abnormally only after the age of three years, sometimes because of an illness such as encephalitis or a slowly developing pathology in the brain, sometimes for no known reason. Diagnosis should be made on the clinical picture. In the view of the present author, age of onset should not be included as an absolute diagnostic criterion.

It is sometimes asked if autism and related conditions are becoming more common. There is no way of answering this question about the past since no prevalence studies were carried out until the first one by Lotter in the 1960s. Careful monitoring and careful application of diagnostic criteria could show any changes that may occur in the future.

TREATMENT

There is as yet no curative treatment. A few possible causes can be prevented, for example immunization can be given against maternal rubella and against some of the virus infections that can affect very young children. Phenylketonuria can be detected at birth and a special diet prescribed. Good ante-natal care is important in preventing obstetric complications. But established autism cannot be cured.

Claims of 'cures'

With any disorder likely to lead to life-long handicaps, from time to time claims are made that a cure has been found which, after a longer or shorter period of time, are found to be false or much exaggerated. Some appear reasonable, at least on the surface but others are to varying degrees unlikely or even bizarre. Autism and related disorders are no exception.

Among the physical treatments suggested are types of medication, special diets and vitamin and mineral supplements. Some parents, who have tried one or other, feel that improvement (not cure) has occurred, others report no effect and yet others believe that the treatment has made the child worse. It may be that different sub-groups of children respond in different ways, but properly controlled scientific evaluation is the only way to obtain answers to the questions raised.

Because most of the affected children appear physically normal,

17

even attractive, and the outward manifestations are in social and emotional behaviour, it is tempting to believe that a purely psychological approach can cure the abnormalities. The isolated skills seem to suggest that, if only some simple key could be found, all would be well. Unfortunately, the underlying impairments are real, severe and have a physical basis in brain function. It is, to say the least, unlikely that they can be repaired by purely psychological approaches. Various forms of psychotherapy and techniques such as holding therapy have been advocated but detailed, controlled evaluation of their effects by independent observers have not yet been published. It must always be remembered that a minority of children who are autistic make good progress without any special treatment. Any therapy must be able to improve on the natural history of the condition for which it is used (see below). This is often overlooked by those making claims for the effectiveness of their own methods.

Education

This cautious approach to treatment claims does not mean that nothing can be done to help the children. It has been shown by independent evaluation that the provision of the right kind of education, management and environment can, as far as possible, minimize handicaps and maximize potential skill. This is the same approach as for any other chronic handicap which cannot be removed. For example, education cannot cure severe visual impairment but it can help a child cope with the world to the best of his ability. The same is true for those with conditions in the autistic continuum.

Medication

Medication can be helpful in reducing high levels of arousal and anxiety, and diminishing challenging behaviour. It does not affect the underlying impairments. It can have undesirable side effects, or even make problems worse. It should therefore be avoided if possible, or used only with caution and stopped if problems occur or when it is no longer necessary.

THE NATURAL HISTORY

Although most remain handicapped all their lives, children with disorders in the autistic continuum do not remain unchanged as they grow from infancy to adulthood. This is one of the reasons why diagnosis can present problems to those familiar only with descriptions of the behaviour found in children around 2–5 years of age with the most typical autism.

The first year

As babies, some of the affected children are remarkably quiet and undemanding. Parents say they did not know they had a baby in the house. Others are restless, irritable and difficult to care for. They may scream through the night and not sleep much in the day either. Many parents of such babies recount how, in despair, they would drive round in the middle of the night because this was the only way to stop the screaming – but the noise would start again immediately the car stopped. Some families never have a peaceful night for years on end and suffer from chronic exhaustion. There are also some babies in whom social impairment becomes evident from around two years or later but whose parents report no special abnormalities in babyhood.

Two to five years

From around 2–5 years, in the children who can walk independently, the impairments usually become very marked, even in those who were quiet as babies. Social isolation or social peculiarity are at their worst, as are the communication problems, and these tend to exacerbate the repetitive and challenging behaviour and the resistance to change. The word 'challenging' suggests to some people that the child is being deliberately naughty. Nothing can be further from the truth. The child finds the world and especially other human beings totally bewildering, and has no idea of the effect of his or her behaviour on other people. This, of course, does not make it any easier for the parents. The poverty of imaginative development means the child has few, or no, constructive activities which adds to all the other difficulties.

The children who are unable to walk independently as well as being socially impaired are, in almost all cases, profoundly physically and mentally handicapped. They are unable to show the repetitive and challenging behaviour of the mobile children but their complete social isolation becomes very evident at the 2–5 year old stage.

Among the mobile group, the overt behaviour pattern and the difficulties of management tend to be fairly similar for all children in the autistic continuum. Psychological testing shows wide variations in patterns of impairments and overall levels of ability, but the problems of the overt behaviour tend to dominate the picture.

It should be noted that there are a minority of socially impaired children who are, on the whole, quiet and amenable, even in the toddler stage, but these are the exceptions to the rule.

Five to ten years

During the years of childhood, from 5 to 10, progress in developmental skills occurs at very different rates in different children. The contrasts among the children in both patterns of skills and overall level of ability begin to become evident in this phase. A few make great strides, giving hopes of eventual normality, others make moderate progress but many show only small gains. However, there is a general tendency for lessening of the challenging behaviour among all the children.

Adolescence

With the advent of the teen-age years and the approach of puberty, a number of the children (it is not known yet precisely how many) have an exacerbation of the behaviour that is characteristic of the autistic continuum, including repetitive activities, resistance to change and aggressive or destructive behaviour. Those who have active but peculiar social approaches to other people may become more demanding and react with anger and aggression if others will not listen, for long periods, to their repetitive talking. Although problems can occur in children of any level of ability, for some of those of higher level of ability, adolescence can be a time of considerable progress in social and intellectual skills and in increasing maturity of behaviour.

Psychiatric problems

Psychiatric complications may be seen in adolescence or early adult life. The most common is depression, especially among those with some awareness of their difference from other people. Those who actively want friends and a sexual partner but lack the social skills to succeed in this are particularly vulnerable to miserable feelings or even a depressive illness. High levels of anxiety can also occur and present problems of management. (The special difficulties to which young people who are more able are particularly prone, are described in Chapter 4.)

Some go through periods of bizarre behaviour, and even what appear to be hallucinations. These are often called psychotic episodes but this adds little to the understanding of the nature of these behavioural breakdowns. They tend to occur when the person concerned feels under pressure, for example if he or she attends a mainstream school and is expected to take exams, or is being bullied by other children. Such episodes rarely, if ever, take the form of typical schizophrenia. They are more like an exacerbation of the confusion about the meaning of everyday experiences which commonly confound people with social impairment.

Epilepsy

By the time of adult life about one third of all socially impaired people have had at least one epileptic fit. These can begin at any time but some occur for the first time at adolescence. There may be only one or two fits and no further problems, or they may continue to occur in adult life.

Treatment of all these complications involves correct diagnosis, exploration of the underlying causes, followed by appropriate environmental management, such as removing sources of stress, personal counselling and, if necessary, medication.

Adult life

After the perturbations of adolescence and early adult life, up to 25 or 30 years, there appears to be a tendency for challenging behaviour to lessen and general cooperativeness to increase. However, the demands of adult life emphasize the great difference

Table 1.2 Adolescents and adults with social impairment*. Outcome at follow-up (age range 16–31 years)

Visuo-spatial IQ	0–49	50–69	70+	Total
(No. in group)	(48)	(20)	(11)	(79)
In residential care (%)	71	25	27	53
Exacerbation in adolescence (%)	35	40	36	37
Currently challenging behaviour (%)	56	30	18	44
Psychiatric complications (%)	8	20	9	11
In open employment (%)	0	0	27	4

*Excluding people who are non-mobile.

in levels of overall ability and the contrasts in quality of social interaction among people who are socially impaired. The results from the follow-up of the children in the Camberwell study described above, illustrate what happens to a complete population of people with social impairment, aged 16–31 years. They are closely similar to those of the few other follow-up studies that have been published.

The 16 non-mobile people showed no change at all in the profound handicaps and five had died by the time of follow-up.

OUTCOME FOR PEOPLE IN THE CAMBERWELL STUDY

As shown in Table 1.2, the group of 79 mobile people with social impairment can be divided according to their ability on tests of visuo-spatial ability obtained in childhood. This gives most of the people concerned the highest estimate of cognitive ability. Nevertheless it is usually the easiest to obtain and the most reliable because the tests are enjoyed and co-operation is good.

It can be seen that outcome is related to the level of visuo-spatial ability. Those with quotients of 70 or above all became more sociable but retained the naivety and oddness characteristic of more able people with social impairment. Three have paid employment of a simple, practical kind. One had been employed but lost his job because of his odd behaviour in social situations. Another young man is likely to find employment when he leaves his further education college. Two live at home and keep themselves occupied with their special interests, visiting libraries to read books on archaeology and space travel respectively. Both of these would like paid employment but have not found jobs as yet, and may well never do so because of their unrealistic ideas. One wanders from place to place, sleeping where he can and has been in trouble with the law because of violent behaviour. Three live in sheltered settings. One has aggressive and destructive behaviour fairly often though he is constructively occupied otherwise. The other two are well settled and work productively.

All of those in the group with quotients in the 50–69 range remained obviously socially impaired though were more sociable than they were as children. Most lived at home and attended day centres whilst the rest were in various forms of residential care. One young man had been in employment but had lost his job because of his inappropriate approaches to girls he met while working. This arose from his desire to have a girl friend. One third retained their severely challenging behaviour.

Those in the group with visuo-spatial quotients below 50 had changed much less than those with more ability. Most remained socially aloof and over half still had severely challenging behaviour. The magnitude of the problems is shown by the fact that over two thirds were in residential care. Those remaining at home needed much supervision and physical care from their parents.

In all the groups, around one third showed exacerbation of challenging behaviour in adolescence, although some improved later. Problems that could be identified as psychiatric conditions occurred in a minority of people. In those who were unable to talk, only marked mood swings or clear physical evidence of tension and anxiety could be identified as psychiatric.

Although all were educated in school, most attended schools for children with severe learning difficulties. Only three went to schools specializing in educating children with autism, and only two are now in units designed for the needs of adults with the same range of conditions.

How to increase and spread the amount of expertise available, and how to find practical ways of applying such knowledge to help children and adults with social impairment of all degrees of severity are challenges that face all of us in this field, parents and professionals alike.

WHAT IS SO SPECIAL ABOUT AUTISM?

On the evidence presented in this chapter, this question should be reworded 'what is so special about social impairment?', since Kanner's autism is but one sub-group among those with impairment of social interaction. Since there are so many different kinds of developmental disorders, in fact as many as there are specific psychological and physical functions contributing to full normal development, why pick out social impairment for special treatment?

Of course, children with any type of developmental delay or disorder need education and special help appropriate to their specific problem or problems. However, social impairment, far more than other such problems, has a particularly devastating effect because it cuts off those affected from the ordinary sources of learning and emotional support other human beings can provide. Unless the nature of their impairments is understood and skilled teaching and caring are provided, the socially impaired people are psychologically isolated in a world they cannot understand.

FURTHER READING

Cohen, D.J., Donnellan, A. and Paul, R. (eds) (1987) *Handbook of Autism and Pervasive Developmental Disorders*, Winston-Wiley, New York.

Coleman, M. and Gillberg, C. (1985) *The Biology of the Autistic Syndromes*, Praeger, New York.

DeMyer, M. (1979) *Parents and Children in Autism*, Winston-Wiley, Washington.

Journal of Autism and Developmental Disorders, issued quarterly by Plenum Press, New York and London.

Kanner, L. (1973) *Childhood Psychosis: Initial Studies and New Insights*, Winston-Wiley, New York.

Schopler, E. and Mesibov, G. (eds) (1988) *Diagnosis and Assessment in Autism*, Plenum, New York.

Wing, L. (ed.) (1988) *Aspects of Autism: Biological Research*, Gaskell, London.

Wing, L. (ed.) (1976) *Early Childhood Autism*, 2nd edn, Pergamon Press, Oxford.

2

The early years

Wendy Brown

There are four aspects of autism, all of which are generally acknowledged to be observable in all children who are autistic. Whilst the extent of the difficulties imposed by the condition may be widely variable, they will all be present to a greater degree than is found in the general population.

These four aspects are:

1. Impaired relationships;
2. Communication difficulties;
3. Obsessionally rigid behaviours;
4. An idiosyncratic, scattered development.

Early and appropriate diagnosis is the first crucial step towards securing a better future for the child who is autistic. Those opposed to 'labelling' children should ask themselves if, when they enter the corner shop, they ask the assistant for a white granular substance which may be used for sweetening cereal, coffee or stewed fruit (even though it is held to increase body weight and damage the hard, sometimes white, chewing, gnawing and gnashing instruments usually found within a major orifice)? Or do they find it practical to ask for a packet of sugar?

Of course there are times when professional people evade labelling for good reasons. Sometimes they avoid it because it is personally painful to be the bearer of bad tidings. Sometimes they are honestly uncertain because, after all, none of us can always be certain of such a very difficult diagnosis, especially one which cannot be verified by a clear-cut, clinical test. We need to share our observations and uncertainties with different disciplines and experiences. 'Truth is a corporate possession. No one of us has all of it!' Professional humility is one of the rarer virtues but autism is happily a great leveller and those closest to the child usually turn out to be the greatest experts.

A label is only the beginning but given the word 'autistic', we should be able to find those people in our own area and all over the country whose expertise and experience can be shared with the child and the whole family.

WHAT DO WE LOOK FOR WHEN WE START WORRYING ABOUT AUTISM?

Impaired relationships

An impaired capacity for making relationships affects all areas of the child's performance, learning and behaviour. It poses difficulties which are both complex and utterly central to the condition. Whilst careful training and the natural process of maturation may bring about improvements, the basic deficit is never wholly curable.

Like other aspects of autism, this quality is very variable. At its most obvious, young children who are autistic appear to fail to distinguish even their parents from other adults; they give the impression of being unseeing, unhearing and unfeeling. Sometimes, however, the child has a bright-eyed intent, direct gaze and will-ingness for physical contact which confuses observers who are unfamiliar with the full spectrum of autistic conditions. Professional people of all disciplines have been known to say, 'he can't be autistic – he smiled at me'. Or, 'he threw his arms around my neck and hugged me'. Or, 'she took my hand and led me to the fridge when she wanted a drink'. Some children with autism will do all of these things. (Not having read Kanner, they don't know they are supposed to eye avoid and shrink from all contact!)

Over a considerable period of time, however, should you observe this 'query autistic child' in the company of other children of the same age, and listen to those who do so daily, you will find that, if the child is autistic, the other children will know this child is different. In subtle or unsubtle ways which they may not be able to define, the child with autism is treating them, not as like-minded people of human value, but as tools, furniture, things to be used. The physical contact which, at first sight, may seem warm is received only on the child's terms, or else in total passivity: it does not come as a response. On close observation, the interaction lacks the range, flexibility or passion the other children bring to physical contact and people who know that child well will be able to tell you so. For instance, when children who are autistic climb onto your lap, they are likely to do so backwards rather than face-to-face, as if getting onto a chair. They won't seek out and respond to the curve of your body or to the mood you are in. They are attending to their own needs, driven by their own moods.

A play-group or nursery class can, therefore, be a really useful place to observe the young child suspected to be autistic. Young children are some of the most reliable and objective informants you will ever find – truthful to a fault – and the experienced staff will have a very clear idea of what constitutes the expected range of behaviours in this age group.

If you are observing a young, very bright boy with autism whose intelligence ensures a very narrow gap is maintained between his performance and that of his peers, a reliable diagnosis is particularly problematic. But there are specific difficulties in this area of relationships which are worth looking out for. For instance, does he reliably know the names of the other children, know who is about to leave for 'big school' and who the boys and who the girls are. You yourself may well be confused by the unisex clothing and hairstyles but the other children will have made it their business to find out. The child who is autistic will have both greater difficulty and less interest in doing so.

Probe too with questions that involve understanding emotion. 'Is Jane happy on that swing do you think?' This involves only a 'yes/no' answer with a 50% chance of seeming to get it right. Leave it open-ended. 'How will Jane feel if I go and push her very high?' is more demanding. You may get the over-literal answer of the young or the child who is autistic ('high', for example) but you may get something far more revealing of the impoverished gaps which are commonly discovered in the autistic mind such as 'go' said by a boy heading for the door in a way which suggests the rest of the sentence has been lost on him. Remember too that a bright child with autism may learn to change the subject long before learning the words, or the concept, 'I don't know', so that this girl may say 'green car now' in response to anything she cannot follow.

Discover who plays with whom and on what terms. Young children with autism may have befrienders but they do not take the initiative in seeking out and sustaining a peer friendship with age-appropriate intensity. At best, the play of young children who are autistic is limited to playing alongside, and at worst, is disruptive,

27

bizarre and sometimes so odd as to be frightening to peers. It lacks symbolism and imagination; it is solitary, rigid and obsessional; and it has more to do with things than with social interaction.

Even under provocation, social interaction can frequently be seen to fail for children who are autistic. For instance, the small boy who has his toy snatched may walk away, cry much later or possibly hit somebody else but, however aggressive he appears to be in other situations of his own initiating, he will very, very seldom successfully stand up for himself with the offender.

The child with autism is also likely to have a greater difficulty than is usual in making choices that relate to and vary with changing circumstances. Most apparent choices (if any are made at all) are likely to adhere to a pattern relating only to itself. For instance, if given hot milk on the first morning at play-group, the child may fail to switch to cold milk in June because whatever the weather, the 'choice' remains fixed.

It may be that any choice has to do with making comparisons, or perceiving the relatedness which makes one thing preferable to another. The fragmented, 'dis-related' mind has great difficulty in doing this. To the very young child with autism, the world is a place of fragmented absolutes. For instance, long past toddlerhood, the child may think of the world as a place where there are babies, children, teenagers and adults, without being able to perceive that the one becomes the other. One 4-year old boy, shown a video of the family, asked who the baby on his mother's lap was. He did not know it was an early film of himself and, although his intellectual capacity was such that he was measurably ahead of his chronological age in reading and writing, he did not seem able to assimilate this concept.

You will not of course need to go into these more complex areas if, when you walk in, you are confronted with a child standing, isolated on the fringes, looking at no one and flicking perseveritively at the wheels of an upside-down car. Just bear in mind that children who are autistic do not all, immediately or always present the classic picture of the disrelated child.

Communication difficulties

Communication difficulties are sometimes difficult to separate from those related to impaired relationships; and they may be equally difficult to pin-point in diagnosis.

The child who has reached the age of three years old, without ever being heard to speak at all, is obviously going to raise anxiety. The child who had fluent early speech and then totally loses it is also going to cause concern. However, there are children whose communication difficulties are less obvious and therefore, once again, an appropriate diagnosis may be delayed. I hope that the following check lists may help illuminate the extent of the actual difficulty for children who may, at first hearing, appear to be communicating in an age-appropriate fashion.

I suggest there are three main areas to examine:

1. Observable difficulties;
2. Delays in normal development;
3. Something referred to here as deviances.

Difficulties

Difficulties which children with all kinds of learning difficulties may have; they will include poor pitch, poor volume control, odd inflexions, cluttering, a robotic quality to the voice, telegrammatic phrases, stammering, stuttering, mispronunciations and articulation problems.

Delays

Delays which, at certain stages, will all be found in children with other difficulties; they include mutism, simple and short-lived echolalia, speaking of oneself in the third person, speaking 'think' as opposed to thinking internally and silently, limitations of vocabulary, limitations in the ability to define words, imprecise word usages, immature syntax, difficulties in understanding prepositions, pronouns, tenses and conjunctions, failures in distinguishing between the animate and the inanimate, and the presence of internalized world models which are not age-appropriate.

All these delays and difficulties may be observed at appropriate ages in young children developing normally. At a later stage than is usual, they may be seen in some children who are autistic. However, there are also areas which would seem to be specifically autistic, which I have called 'deviant'. Others may wish to use another term. Not all 'deviances' will be observed in every child with autism but they are unlikely to be observed to any appreciable extent, beyond the appropriate age, in children with other kinds of learning difficulties.

29

Deviances

Deviances may include:

1. *An impaired motivation* to communicate spontaneously and interpersonally. Most people actually want to talk to others quite a lot of the time. 'Birds have wings because they fly'. People, it may be argued, have speech because they are motivated to communicate. Yet children with autism who have been taught some speech may totally fail to use it, even when it is not merely appropriate but to their personal advantage to do so. Or they may use it only at the instigation or on the insistence of an adult, and then with as little effort or skill as the adult allows. This applies as much to sign languages as to speech.

This impaired motivation affects the ability of children with autism to initiate and foster relationships at all levels. It may be used to block out another speaker when it would be usual to respond. It is associated with a failure to establish, or apparently even a need to know or take account of, the sex of the person with whom they are speaking.

Some children may display ignorance of the concept that effective communication consists of a 'two-way traffic'. Taking conversational turns, which very young babies have been observed to do, often has to be taught and then is only mechanically learned by some children who are autistic. Experiences or emotions are infrequently shared spontaneously with other people.

Nor is effective communication seen to be interpersonal. For instance, one non-speaking child signed for help to a toilet wall when she could not undress easily. Another delivered a verbal message, as taught, to an empty room when the person who should have been there to receive it had gone out.

2. *Deviance in syntax* such as 'put it on shoe' meaning 'please will you put my shoe on for me?' These forms may be so personalized and entrenched that they are used throughout life, resistant to all attempts at correction.

3. *Pronoun reversal* – the classic 'would you like a biscuit?' meaning 'I want a biscuit'. Again this usage may be highly resistant to correction.

4. *Echolalia – simple and delayed, appropriate and inappropriate* – sometimes echoed speech is heard which is meaningful

at the time, or later. It may have some association with the present situation, or an earlier one, or the association may be obscure or apparently non-existent. Sometimes, in relation to the child, the echoed speech seems quite devoid of meaning, experience or reality – it is merely an acquired repetition of no remembered significance or source. And, there are instances where a child will appear to 'recite' details of an event in which he or she did not take any part, even as an observer.

Sometimes, there is an echoed phrase which appears to be part of some ritual. For instance, a particular child under stress would always say 'oranges and lemons, oranges and lemons . . . ' Another child sang 'post the letter, post the letter', but did not 'see' the red box in front of her.

5. *An obsessively limited and inflexible subject range* which may not easily lend itself to direction or extension. For instance, one child asked every visitor to her school, 'can I plunge your sink?' She would then rush outside to see water coming through a drain, 'where does the water go?' was the next question. Yet neither of these questions ever incorporated answers or extensions such as information given on drains, waterways, and so on.

6. *Failure in understanding situations* which most children are able to use to advance and learn by both verbal and non-verbal means, whether taught or not. One fastidious child, with a measurably high IQ, walked into heavy mud in his socks the day his boots were not in their usual place. He appeared to dislike this but did not appear to know what to do about it. An older child, noticing that a bridge was lit up, said it was 'so the bridge could see better'. Another child told to stand in a queue did so but did not move up with it.

7. *Failures in transposing language* so that, from another's viewpoint, it is acquired inappropriately. For instance, a phobic child in a state of rising panic at the sight of a dog may say, 'it's a lovely doggie. It won't hurt you'. This is said on a revealing note of rising panic. The child appears to be using the words not as reassurance as the original speaker intended (possibly some considerable time ago) but as an expression of acute fear.

8. *Significantly different perception.* Rather than looking at the obvious 'whole' picture, a child may appear to see in small, fragmented, peripheral ways so that, given a large poster of a house

and asked to comment, the child with autism says 'push-chair', referring to the tiny object tucked away at one side.

9. *Compulsive questioning* for which some ritualized answer is required or for which no answer or response is required, or which is persistently carried out because, however framed or demonstrated, the child does not appear to be able to assimilate the answer. Since to be able to frame a question is usually to be more than half-way to being able to understand the reply, for all other young children it is safe to assume questions should be answered. Sadly, this is by no means always the case with children who are autistic.

10. *Using word association* as a response to questioning, or as a form of interaction. This can be very misleading as it is often quite divorced from the child's real experience. One boy was asked what he had for breakfast. He picked up the last word and responded 'cornflakes'. A less experienced questioner may have accepted this as fact. In an attempt to extend the conversation with this child who had a good vocabulary, his worker then said 'what else?' He went on, 'weetabix, shredded wheat, muesli . . .' 'No', she said, 'this morning, what did you have this morning?' 'Toast?' 'Very good . . .' 'Toast, baps, bread, sandwiches, ryvita . . .'.

Much of the time, children who are autistic aim to please. They are not tied to our reality. Much of the language we offer them is little understood. Words fly at them. They trade them back as best they can . . . they are not lying just trying!

11. *Acquiring parental accent, intonation and vocabulary.* For most children, there is a strong desire to acquire uniformity with the peer group. Through inflexibility of learning and ignorance of the very existence of a peer group, it can happen that the boy who is autistic, though brought up in Wales, speaks with a strong Northern accent if this is what his parents do at home.

12. *Over-literal interpretations* which lead to such misunderstandings as washing hands in the toilet pan when told to 'go to the toilet and wash your hands'.

Overall, there is a great difficulty with abstract concepts, assumptions and inferences. It led to one gifted teacher saying 'If you can't touch it, see it, hear it, smell it, taste it, then don't try teaching it!'

13. *Saying what they do not understand* – this can be very

convincing (and misleading) unless you know the child well enough to establish where the reality is. For example, older child, 'did you hear the telephone ring? I think I did . . .' Teacher, 'no' Child, 'are you sure? I could have sworn I heard it' Teacher, 'quite sure?' They were both standing on top of a tor in the middle of Dartmoor. This anecdote is not an isolated occurrence of this child sounding utterly plausible in a whole range of meaningless contexts.

Obsessionally rigid behaviours

Of course we are all obsessional, clinging to our favourite routines, places and people, our cups of tea with or without milk, one sugar or two, and so on. Young children especially cling to what they know. Not many of us adults are enamoured of change either, especially changes we have not initiated or been consulted about.
Children who are autistic, however, may carry these behaviours to greater lengths than is usual. Sometimes it seems that obsessions are the most motivating influence in their lives, perhaps the only motivation. They can affect the whole day as well as essential routines such as eating, sleeping, toilet-training and general management. They may include self-mutilation, the collecting of bizarre objects no one dares discourage, turning and spinning objects – or the child him or herself, repeating tasks, refusing to accept changes outside the familiar, mannerisms which mark out an otherwise normal-looking child from others, rituals, pica, destructive actions, possibly aggressive and anti-social actions.

Despite the nature and range of the difficulties listed, it can be an aspect of autism on which surprisingly little reliable information may be forthcoming. If the informant is the nursery teacher, or play-group leader, this may be because, within a new environment, the claims of the tyrannical newcomer have not yet been established.

If the parent is the informant, it may be that utter exhaustion has led to the line of least resistance being adopted. The mother may have ceased to be aware that she always gives the child a particular mug, crosses the street in the same place, sings all the nursery rhymes in the same order. After all, it is much easier to condition a 'normal' parent than a child who is autistic. Moreover, many parents may see these behaviours as real and preferred choices, as something they do which is a positive way of giving to their young stranger. He may not want the newest and flashiest tricycle available, but he does so love his old blue pyjama jacket on in the sand-pit. And why not?

Awareness of the inflexibility of a child's behaviours may be revealed by probing questions or perhaps only after long months of trained observation. It may be a great problem, or something which can be used constructively, or merely a minor foible. The range, as with everything concerning autism, is very great.

Idiosyncratic scattered development

This can be a really useful diagnostic tool, since it may differentiate the child who is autistic from the child who is more globally delayed.

Typically, within the group of children affected by the spectrum of autistic conditions, the child who has very severe, additional learning difficulties and whose other skills are delayed will nevertheless have acquired one skill that is outside the expected range, such as kicking and catching a ball.

For children whose disabilities place them in the middle of the spectrum, it can be a deciding factor on school placement, since some skills are likely to be fostered more easily in one environment than another.

Diagnosis at the upper end of the spectrum of autistic conditions can be complicated. Parents and professionals may see the child as gifted, as choosing not to respond to simple tasks or unwanted instruction, and as using divergent thought to communicate original ideas. It should be remembered that the truly gifted child is able in almost all areas of development, whereas the child with autism will have narrow and obsessional skills and a number of contrasting delays.

People tend to think of these idiosyncrasies in terms of the popular phrase, 'islets of ability'. For every gifted artist or musician, however, there are many more children whose key-workers are perplexed by the unevenness of their highly individual development. This manifests itself in an ability to learn the colour turquoise whilst failing to learn red, or in picking out by name a toy hippopotamus but not a sweet or a cup or a familiar and apparently liked adult.

HOW DOES ALL THIS MAKE US FEEL?

When a child's behaviour runs counter to our training and expectations, it may appear wilful. However, there is no evidence to support an assumption we have no right, consciously or unconsciously, to make.

Nevertheless, the peculiarities of learning and development, the communication difficulties, and the impaired capacity for relationships do affect the way we all feel about the child. Even parents, with their longed-for first-born, can feel a sense of rejection and, as for the rest of us, we can be made to feel wholly incompetent and out of our professional depth.

Of course we should all like to know why. Sometimes, after all the 'why's' have been properly considered, we have to accept that we cannot find all the answers. Then we have to try to find ways of living with not knowing. Because we cannot cure, we have to live with failure too, with not being good enough. In that situation, it is human to want to allocate blame. Parents blame themselves or each other and professionals do all that too. It is common enough but not constructive.

Fortunately, there is another aspect of autism known best to those who are devoted to a particular child or group of children. It is an endearing innocence which children who are autistic never out-grow and which ensures them a very fair supply of tender loving care.

AND HOW DO THE CHILDREN FEEL?

In the great majority of cases, autism protects children from insight. On their own terms, in their own way, with no contrasting picture in their minds of how life might have been, they can, in the right place and with appropriate support, have fun and be fun.

SUPPORTING THE CHILD

When spontaneous development fails, training is the next best thing. Whatever the extent of the child's disability, we need to intrude early upon the autism, with a positive, planned and personal programme of intervention.

A good starting-point is the principle that everything this child needs to do and to know will have to be taught. In defiance of our training and previous experience, some things will have to be learnt both without understanding and outside the normal sequence of development.

Of course, this particular child's readiness must first be evaluated. What is the child ready to learn now and what is the first step towards teaching it – these are the useful questions. Almost all teaching, real teaching (by which I mean the acquisition of a wholly new skill by a child) will only be possible given a 1:1 teacher/child ratio. Children with autism proceed at their own pace, in their own idiosyncratic fashion. How anything is learnt is often highly personal. For the greater part of the day then, it is imperative to provide individual programmes.

For this child, at this time, the chosen tasks, skills or occupation need to have value in themselves. What you teach is what the child learns. Be more than half-sure that the selected task can be performed. Do not put the child who is autistic in the position of the child who is blind with a picture book. Sadly, there are aspects of an ordinary childhood – like symbolic and imaginative play – which are frequently not within the child's reach, whereas putting on his or her socks or reading a sentence may be less than half a step away. Be realistic about this.

Sometimes frustrated workers say, 'I really think he could if only he would . . .'. But, thinking in unproveable terms of 'will he or can't he, and which is which?' is not useful. It is more practical to ask what the child does or does not do. What he doesn't do for whatever reason, gives you some guide-lines about his limitations.

Don't allow yourself to get punitive because this child's good looks are at variance with what he does. He needs all the positives you can give him. Remember that what he needs is teaching and don't confuse that with testing. Testing is sitting back observing mistakes being made. Teaching is setting up a programme for the child to get it right and to go on and on getting it right. This child learns what he does. If you give him the opportunity to make mistakes, he will learn the mistakes.

Don't ask this child to perform a task again and again and again so that he is in the situation of getting it wrong seven times over before you put it all away with a 'good boy' when he gets it right the last time – just the once. Put him in a situation where he gets it right seven times.

There is much that is difficult in teaching a child with autism. That very difficulty is the challenge which attracts and holds the attention of a great many people in a field which is always stimulating and never dull.

SUPPORT IN SPECIFIC AREAS OF DIFFICULTY

Impaired relationships

I would not myself spend time in working directly on relationship-forming, or indeed on making eye contact. Choose a practical task which is useful to the child in its own right. When you can help this child to succeed tangibly then you have something to build on. Relationships between people are often closest when collectively engaged on some project and children with autism are often most attached to the key-workers who have taught them to eat a new food or perform a set task. Increased confidence and mutual trust improve the ability to stay on task, to look at that task and to seek out the person who taught it.

The way the rest of the world relates to the child can be improved by teaching as many social niceties as possible. The child will not see the point of 'please' or of using a knife and fork but others will respond with pleasure and that will help to get the child a fairer deal.

These are children who need our help to ensure they conform as much as they can in social ways, so that options are kept open. On the whole, because they may take a long time to learn (and then they will stick to the rules with a tenacious rigidity which replaces understanding), it is useful to say that if what they do now will not be acceptable at 20 then it is probably better to start restricting it at two.

Teaching privacy can hardly begin too early. Some families find it natural to wander round the home, between shower and bedroom, with nothing on. Or, they may conduct a family conversation from the toilet with the door open. Many of us do these things with our youngest children, at that time when they still seem to be so much part of us. Sadly, as they grow older and move into unfamiliar situations and places, some young people with autism are bewildered when they continue to do what they have always been allowed to do at home. Families need to know that it is precisely because children who are autistic won't know what you are teaching (much less why) that you do need to insist they stay in the toilet to re-dress themselves, that they keep the door at least half-way shut and their swim-suits on on the beach – even though their wetness offends them – and so on.

All young children are sexual beings. They handle their genitals in a spirit of enquiry and pleasure. They put their fingers into their own orifices and other peoples' (and they are not offended by what they find there). They do this in the High Street and when auntie comes to tea.

What a family chooses to do about this for any child is highly individual but what you have to remember is that the child who is autistic lacks empathy and inhibition. This child is motivated more by obsessional drives than by any other single factor. They like what they do. They may like it even more if auntie turns an interesting shade while they're doing it. They are not open to sweet reason or talking it through. Quietly find them something else to do – preferably more interesting, if that's possible. Find a way of stopping them that does not raise the emotional temperature and learn not to worry about things which have not happened.

Communication difficulties

Very basic, early communication often begins as a form of imitation. Young children with autism can be taught to imitate by having one adult demonstrating perhaps a clapping action in front of the child, while another adult stands behind, moving the child's hands into the necessary position and guiding them through the movements. Once the child grasps what is required, this support may be faded out. The child may then be encouraged to engage in a range of interactive games such as peek-a-boo, patacake, and so on.

Imitation and cooperation are the first, vital ingredients. They need to be rewarded with anything you can find that works for this child. At first, you may need physically to manipulate the child through 'sit down' in order to have something to reward. Whether or not there is speech, the degree to which the child is able to understand is vitally important and often lends itself to direct, repetitive teaching. Despite their bright-eyed, knowing look, children who are autistic seldom understand everything that is said to them. A speech therapist should be able to help assess the difficulties and advise on ways of increasing understanding, promoting the labelling of everyday objects and encouraging a response to brief, concrete instructions. Sometimes, visual as well as spoken clues may help children who cannot speak but who demonstrate understanding of spoken instructions such as 'give me the cup'. They may be taught to 'read' and write a number of words they cannot say. It is a possibility worth exploring.

Many parents will ask, if the child cannot speak what about sign language? For some children, the British Sign Language (Makaton vocabulary individually adapted) can be useful. It should always be tried. In general, the children most likely to make most progress with signing are children whose understanding is in advance of their ability to utter meaningful sounds. Moreover, they actually want to communicate or are easily rewarded for doing so. These children can make very real progress, in a way which is both practically useful and intensely satisfying to the children themselves. It may (especially perhaps if the child has an additional hearing loss) be combined with lip-reading, writing and reading.

However, there are a number of children whose cognitive development is so delayed that signing is as inaccessible to them as the spoken word. They may learn to repeat one or two signs when cued, but they fail to relate this to meaning and, however consistent the input, use them spontaneously. That is not to say that signing should not be tried or that it should not be tried over a long period and then tried again at different times in the child's life. It must be said, however, that sign language is not always the longed-for answer to profound communication difficulties we would all wish it to be.

At all stages, learn to limit your own language appropriately and to use 'autese', that is words which, from this child's own viewpoint, are most likely to be understood. In this way, if the child echoes them back, they can be understood. Consider this example, 'come on sunshine, let's get out and see how the world goes. We'll put your shoes on, shall we? Here we go then, one on this little piggy and the other on that. . . .' Now translate that into autese and you get (in a nice firm voice on a downward note of confident command) 'Kevin. Shoes on. Good boy. Out we go.' Fit the actions to the words.

Don't overload and don't over-extend. Don't give reasons that this child cannot understand. It leads to what I call the 'cauzee syndrome'. We had one lad very conditioned to following up every instruction with the question, 'cauzee?' So we had, 'Put your coat on, Michael'. 'Cauzee?' 'Because you are going out and it's cold today.' Satisfied, Michael murmurs, 'Cauzee cold out'. Michael is satisfied because we have supplied the missing piece of his verbal jigsaw, the piece his obsessional nature craves and which we have taught him to expect. But if Michael could tell us what he felt, it might go like this. 'Cold? Out? I'm in and it's warm. What's she

39

on about?' We have robbed reason of being reasonable by imposing a future condition on a child who can only feel in the here and now.

We need to be careful too not to ask questions to which children do not have any immediate and concrete access. 'What did you do at the weekend?' Where is this 'weekend' to young children with autism? Can you put a picture of it in their minds, or press a button which enables them to do so? If you supply a verbal answer, divorced from any literal meaning, you are once again teaching them that language is a meaningless exercise. Do not then be surprised if, in later years, they talk about a trip to the zoo they never had.

Obsessions and other behavioural difficulties

In very general terms, all these problems tend to be at their most excessive in their most familiar context. For most young children, this will of course be home. Since behaviour patterns are very specific in nature, they may not be transferred to a new situation: a school may be blissfully unaware of the constrictions being imposed on the family by a young tyrant. In time, however, the child's attention will be turned on what is familiar in the classroom.

Intervention is the name of the game. Obsessions are self-perpetuating. Children who are autistic like what they do. If you are not continually controlling, limiting, forbidding the obsession it will come to dominate and place handicapping limitations on their entire lives. We may need to over-direct in ways which would be unacceptable with other children.

Take food for instance. Many young children are very limited in their choices but, as they grow up and want to explore and keep up with their peers, they become more flexible. The young child with autism is only likely to change if someone specifically sets out to bring that change about. With this child, everything is the thin end of an invisible wedge. The 3-year old who refuses carrots and gets away with it may end up living on one particular brand of pineapples for years on end.

The simplest rules are of course the most easily taught. In other words, you need the kind of regime which can dictate: 'we always eat every single thing on our plate. Nothing is left'. Making what may seem like reasonable exceptions, being flexible in ways which are appropriate for other youngsters, only confuses children who are autistic. If the rule is a clean plate then don't make an exception for pickled onions. Children with these difficulties just won't understand.

Direct them or they will direct you and their lives will be impoverished for that.

To take another example, let us look at this girl's behaviour in the sand-pit. Does she always dribble sand through her left hand? That may be because no one has insisted on showing her she can do it through a sieve or a plastic jug, or indeed that there are numerous other things to be done with sand. If the obsession cannot be usefully extended, perhaps you may be able to use it as a reward. 'Sit on your pot for two minutes and I'll let you dribble sand through your left hand'. (Of course this, as with so much, is not a spoken negotiation but one taught through direct, repeated and well-timed action.) Perhaps the problem is that she is insisting on dribbling sand when you want her at the table, or out of the door, or in the bathroom. In that case, just take the sand away.

The most difficult obsessions to tackle are those which cannot be removed when all else fails. Screaming, self-mutilation, aggression are just such behaviours. With screaming you can pretend not to hear. That is the nearest you can get to taking sound away. But that is easier to write than to do. Your wincing eyes will give you away. It is also more easily done, during the day, by a group of professional people, able to give each other group support.

Never, never let a small child get something by screaming. Rewarding it may seem easy but, in the long run, it never is. Never. That may be obvious, something we all know, but common sense can fly out of the window when an exhausted parent, who may pity the child for his or her handicap, has been up all night. Perhaps the worst bit is not knowing when it will stop, why it is happening, or what triggered it off in the first place. Protracted screaming, with no known pattern or cause, requires immediate, practical support for the carer, or the child may well be at risk.

Sometimes, it is as if the behaviour of young children contains an element of cunning manipulation, evil in intent. It rouses strong feelings in professionals and parents alike. Perhaps it is because the inhibitory influence of empathy is lacking that, with apparently total disregard for any pain caused, children who are autistic are capable of using other people to satisfy their needs. Whatever the reason, it is a phenomenon often observed by key-workers, especially the closest key-workers of all, the child's parents.

When children seem 'out to get you', when they behave as if they want to hurt you and apparently know how, then what is really surprising is the number of families who continue to support each other and their children. Of course, we cannot know what young

41

children who are autistic feel when they scream at a piece of dust, smile at the doctor giving them an injection, or pursue their monologues about who won the Derby in 1972 as a lump of snow slides down their back. How much less can we claim to know what this child feels (or thinks we feel) as, with a gleeful smile lighting his face, he hurls auntie's handbag through the window?

This is not to suggest that you can or should do nothing about the behaviour, merely that your effective counter-action needs to be humanely rooted in the understanding that you are dealing with a handicap, not with malevolence.

Idiosyncratic development

Exploit this one where you can. Let both child and family enjoy any special skills there may be. Professional people can use this feature diagnostically, not only to identify autism, but to help choose what kind of school is going to be most suitable for which child. Perhaps I can clarify that latter statement by looking at four children.

Eric

Eric has a measurably higher than average intelligence, even at this young pre-school age, and certain useful communication skills. His behaviour patterns are not too unusual for a young child. Ideally, he should go into a nursery or play-group with other young children – preferably from the age of two.

We shall be looking for a small group, with a high staff ratio, so that through the day Eric can have as much individual support as he demonstrates he needs. The staff need to be both sympathetic to his idiosyncrasies and firm when the need for modification and conformity is perceived. Time should be spent in getting on friendly terms with the other parents to increase both their understanding and that of their children of Eric's special difficulties. If the other children do not understand Eric, they may be frightened of him and none of us behave well when we are frightened. Eric does not have to behave outlandishly to provoke this alienation, he just has to be different. Anything a little off-centre raises our anxiety. The help of the social worker, health visitor, speech therapist, child guidance clinic, psychiatrist, educational and/or clinical psychologist, and doctor should be enlisted. In whatever way it is offered.

When the time comes for Eric to leave this group a small, friendly and caring infant school, with small classes, should be sought. Auxiliary help from the local education authority may be required. The small, possibly private, old-fashioned primary school, where children actually sit at desks and do what they are told to do for most of the day, should be seriously considered. Little thinking is involved and, in my view, although quite inappropriate for most infants, it may suit Eric very well. He needs more direction and control than is usual. He is likely to learn to read and write easily, but he will not have any idea how to occupy himself appropriately in the playground or at dinner-time. He may work only to cue, need cueing for the toilet, and require someone to watch over him to see that other children respond to him kindly.

Jean

Jean's measurable intelligence falls within the range shared by the group of children recognized as having moderate learning difficulties. Her behaviour is generally acceptable and she has some communication skills (but is nowhere near as fluent as Eric). She might manage in the same pre-school group as Eric or, depending on what is available in her area, she may do better in a group which specializes in teaching and managing children with many kinds of learning difficulties. This decision can only be made by visiting, discussing and observing what happens in different settings. In general terms, I myself would be wary of any professional person who is at all touchy about being observed or assessed with a view to providing a suitable placement for this child. Good communication, essential for all those concerned with a child who is handicapped, does so often depend on the attitude of key individuals. You need to be able to deal with all the difficulties openly and honestly.

At five years old, Jean may go on to a school for children with moderate learning difficulties or to a school for other children with autism. It depends on what is available and how much help Jean needs, on an individual basis, to make the curriculum of the school accessible to her. And the curriculum itself needs looking at. Is it appropriate for Jean? Or will she be in the position of that blind child sitting looking at picture books all day? Remember that Jean's communication difficulties are such that she will only benefit from individual instruction, including even such simple requests as 'go out to play now'. Will this be available for her?

William

William is very delayed in all aspects of his development and has distinct autistic features. He would probably be much happier meeting the expectations of staff who are used to teaching and managing children with severe learning difficulties. It may not be appropriate to pressurize him to learn things for which, at this time, he is not yet ready. Despite his bright good looks, everyone needs to learn to think of his performance as that of a much younger child. At five years old, his skills are more like those of a one-year old and he will need to be in a school where there are other children with severe learning difficulties. Or, if available, a school for other children with autism, where staff are used to the dual handicap. When making a decision about placement, we need, as before, to take into consideration the suitability and accessibility of the curriculum, staffing levels, and the communication skills and good will of the staff.

Rose

Rose's behaviour causes severe problems. She may have a high intelligence, or very severe learning difficulties, or be somewhere in-between but what concerns all her key-workers most is the difficulty they have in managing her behaviour. She cannot be contained in a play-group or nursery and it is going to be difficult to place her in a school at five.

Rose's family are already under terrible strain and crisis intervention is called for. Key-workers may need to work with Rose on a rota system, spending relatively short periods with her. She may need a continuous, one-to-one ratio or it may not be thought safe to leave only one person with her at any one time, either for her safety or for theirs.

Children whose behaviours provoke stress need safeguards. Shared care may have to be sought because, at the time of writing, resources for such children are very thinly stretched. Sometimes, even at this age, very sadly a child may go from short-term residential care, to a foster home, back to the family and into a play-group, as well as attending a nursery part-time. Whilst this is not ideal, it is an evasion of reality to suggest that these circumstances are in all cases causal. They may well be bad for the child and require a more appropriate remedy but a child in 'triangular care' tends to be there because of his or her behaviour and not vice versa.

Whatever the difficulties or successes in placing Eric, Jean, William and Rose, for all children who are autistic there needs, at all stages of their lives, to be a key-worker or parent substitute. Someone needs to have worked out what these children (who do not always say what they mean or mean what they say) actually mean. Someone needs to really like them. Someone needs to see that they are different and the staff as a group need to be quite clear that the environment is geared to striving for the best these children are capable of, at a pace to suit their needs.

Being autistic means being highly individual. Scattered development alone means having a pattern of development which is not just different from the norm but is different from that of all other children who are autistic. There is seldom a time when any group of children with autism, however small and however carefully selected, can be usefully taught 'as a group'. Whatever the setting, one child's needs are different from the others in terms of communication, play, eating, occupation, teaching, relating, learning, forming rules and making choices. It adds up to a personalized curriculum for each child.

Schools set up for children with autism do have some advantages, for some children, for some of the time. There are likely to be more rules than would generally be the case. The philosophy of intervention can be more consistently applied. Parents are less isolated. The staff ratio is often more favourable. And the school ethos enables teachers to assume that a class of six children equals not one class but six individual classes. The curriculum itself has been worked out with autism as the starting point. The peculiarities of 'autese' have been lived with and, bearing in mind that it can take something like 2 years of living with autism to begin to understand the condition, that is a considerable advantage.

But wherever you visit, look for a sense of purpose, humour, flexibility and happiness. Ask yourself, do the staff like the children? And each other? Do you like them? Do they work hard? Are they lively and imaginative? Do they want to understand autism? Will they try and understand Jean, Rose, William and Eric, and are they committed to getting the best out of them? Will they intervene on autism as much as is reasonable and will they tolerate lovingly what they cannot alter? Will Eric, William, Rose and Jean spend a major part of the day doing what makes sense to them, or will they be expected to tag along, on the fringe of a group, conforming to what they cannot share?

SUPPORTING THE CARERS

The parent alone

Inevitably, during these early years, some parents will find themselves alone with this child a very great deal of the time. Even if the school, nursery or play-group is very good indeed, there are still long holidays, weekends and evenings.

If home programming is available from any source at all, it is well worth offering parents professional advice. Some families find it helpful, others threatening but, whatever the decision, the opportunity should be made available. Parent and child will fare better if pity can be put on one side and normal guidelines aimed at which are fair to both. For a start, 'no' must mean just that. No is not negotiable.

Teaching the young child who is autistic can be exciting for both concerned. Patience, persistence, insight and ingenuity are all called for. The starting-point will always be, what do other children of this age do? Can I initiate one of those activities?

Teachers, however, get time off – rather a lot according to some. If the parent has to become this child's teacher (and for a child with learning problems, at least some of the time that must be so) then the adult too needs time off from the intensity involved. Parents may need to be helped to be kind to themselves. Survival, even more than intervention, is the name of the game.

Parents and professionals together

Of course we would all like to assume that the child comes first and parents and professionals will work together to meet the child's needs. But, if the community is to care, then the community needs to be informed and involved and we all have to play some part in that.

Sadly, most resources are thinly stretched and frequently operating at crisis level. This may mean that they are being used for those who shout the loudest not those with the stiffest upper lip. Parents need professional people to support them in getting what help is available and helping them accept help which is less than ideal.

Comments like these are all too common. 'My GP's never seen her'. 'That teacher doesn't want her in his school'. 'My neighbours don't talk to me – not since they reported me to the NSPCC when she was screaming.' 'My social worker did come – well, I'll give anyone a cup of tea. Asked me what I wanted – a ball and chain to keep him in, I said. Well, she's not been back.' 'That speech therapist, she just gave her a doll to play with – well, she doesn't play, does she?'

There is an art in using what is available and all these professional people do have their uses. They need to be cultivated, informed, trained, nurtured. But the people who need them most may be least able, in their exhausted and grief-stricken state, to approach others positively.

All of us concerned with the child's family, in whatever capacity, need to know that, in these early years, we are dealing with a bereavement. If we are the first to suggest that all may not be well we are, in effect, announcing the death of the child they thought they had. Normal parents' expectations are normal. The reality of their child may be profoundly shocking. However practically helpful any carer tries to be, at this time, being the nearest person may mean getting kicked. We need to know that and to find the resources to cope. Round the table, frank discussion is needed to sort out what is constructive, reasonable criticism from what is an expression of fear, anger and frustration.

Sometimes, in wholly realistic terms, a parent is squeamish about allowing a difficult child to go to unsuspecting strangers who have seen only big blue eyes and curly-haired innocence, smiling sweetly out of the window. It is difficult to explain autism to the uninitiated, not merely because the child looks normal, but because what you are trying to communicate is outside ordinary experience. It can seem like coming back from another planet and describing a colour which does not exist on earth. People can only relate what you are saying to what they already know, and as previously suggested, no one really knows about autism until they have lived with it for at least two years.

The parents' distrust, therefore, is reasonable but a long-term view nevertheless needs to be thought through. None are more quickly converted to believing in the condition than those who have had to care for a child with autism for any length of time. It is ultimately in everyone's interests to let the willing care worker take the child for a walk, the classroom assistant have her for a weekend, or Granny spend the evening sitting. Of course there will be mistakes. Few people are prepared for the incredible speed, determination and strength of the child. There is, however, a rich harvest to be gained in terms of understanding and empathy. The new carer may even get good at it and become hooked for life. (There are a lot of us about.)

In terms of parental morale, it is hard when the child behaves well! Granny, teacher, friend, beware. Do not boost your own ego at the expense of the child's parents. All children have times when they behave worse with their own parents. It isn't nice but it happens.

Some children behave totally differently in a different place with a different person. It takes a good deal of mutual trust and good communication for involved adults to accept that this is part of autism rather than degrees of competence or simply misinformation.

Whatever the decisions which have to be reached about this child, all professional people should listen to the key-workers – those closest to the child for the longest period of time. Yet it sometimes seems we have a very curious hierarchy of expertise which goes something like this. The mother who has been with the child since birth and often provides the most care, in every sense of that word, is treated somewhat dismissively. She is both untrained and emotionally involved. The untrained classroom auxiliary who tends the child for hours each day may well get the same treatment. The teacher, although often less intimately involved, may fare better. The psychologist on the other hand, who has perhaps assessed the child once, is listened to with respect. And we pay even more attention to the psychiatrist who has perhaps met the child on one, highly atypical occasion.

I once entertained a dozen young doctors in training. They were asked to observe one child each in the nursery. In discussion, it emerged that what had bothered them most during their visit was not being introduced to the other adults present in the room. 'Why?' 'Because we didn't know who they were – teachers, parents, classroom assistant . . .' 'Why did you need to know that – you were observing a child . . .' 'Well, we'd have – treated them – differently . . .' Perhaps you shouldn't.

In conclusion I would underline my plea for honest communication, however painful. Parents may not like professional people asking them to consider a referral for diagnosis. They may not like the diagnosis but it is the first step towards obtaining appropriate help. Situations do arise and may persist for years in which a conspiracy of silence is maintained, to the extent that the only person concerned with the child who does not know that autism is under consideration is the parent.

FURTHER READING

Carr, J. (1980) *Helping Your Handicapped Child*, Penguin, London.
Wing, L. (1980) *Autistic Children*, Constable, London.

3

The years between 6 and 12

Rita Jordan

The years between 6 and 12 have often been described as the 'honeymoon' period in the lives of children with autism and their families. At home, some form of acceptable (if bizarre) harmony has been achieved; the early traumas of diagnosis, the most violent of the temper tantrums and bouts of hyperactivity have usually passed. The re-emergence of frustration and emotional disturbance that may accompany the hormonal changes of adolescence have yet to come.

The focus of attention and concern in the first part of this period is on obtaining the appropriate education to meet the child's needs. This may remain a cause for concern throughout these years as the very special needs of the child gradually become more apparent. The quality of life for both child and family may well depend on how successfully these needs are being met and how far management strategies that are working in the school setting can be transferred to the home. Where education is provided on a day basis, the need for some form of respite is likely to persist.

Pressure on the families remains high. Even where children do not present difficult or unmanageable behaviours, the need for vigilance in monitoring self-help and social skills persists, however able the child. Their failure to develop interests and engage in purposeful activity, coupled with the need to limit and control their excessive obsessional concerns, means that families continue to have the prime responsibility for organizing and managing their leisure time – this at a stage when other children would be developing interests outside the home.

These problems are exacerbated by the difficulties of peer interaction experienced by children with autism, and their consequent lack of friends. The overall result is a significant need to find some way of occupying the long out-of-school hours. Persistent communication difficulties, regardless of the level of linguistic ability achieved, only serve to create further problems for child and family.

EDUCATIONAL PLACEMENT

The initial factor affecting educational placement is time of diagnosis; if the child's problems are severe, diagnosis is likely to have been made in the pre-school years. Decisions on appropriate placement will then be made on the basis of assessed educational need, in the light of the provision made by the local educational authority.

The 1981 Education Act requires an assessment to be made on any child (two years or over, and in some cases from birth) who, there is reason to believe has, or will have on entering school, special educational needs that cannot be met within the normal resources available in that authority. Following assessment, in which evidence is collected both from parents and from medical, educational, psychological and other relevant professional advisers, a statement detailing the child's special educational needs and the provision necessary to meet those needs, is drawn up. This is presented to the parents for comment and, ultimately, agreement, although there is a statutory period of time during which parents can meet with local education officers to raise any objections they have about the content of the statement. Parents have the right of appeal first to an Appeals Committee and then to the Secretary of State but they need to provide evidence either of incorrect assessment of need, or that the suggested provision will not meet those needs.

Because the 1981 Act abolished medical categories as a basis for determining educational need, a diagnosis of autism (to obtain which may have involved a fight to find the right professional) will not of itself guarantee either recognition of the specific needs of the child with autism or any form of specialist provision. Once again parents may have a battle to find the professional with sufficient experience and expertise both to identify the educational needs of the child and to suggest appropriate provision.

The task of finding a setting – acceptable to the local education authority – where that provision can be made, remains. Conflict arises when the priorities of the education authorities do not match those of the parents or concerned professionals. Specialist provision is expensive, whereas the authority has a duty to consider overall allocation of resources as well as the needs of individual children.

Not all children who are autistic are diagnosed before entering school. Sometimes the problems of bright children with autism are not apparent until they are in the social environment of a school. Here, unlike the more flexible home environment, where unwitting adaptations to the requirements of the child with autism may well have been made, they are required to conform to the standards of others.

Other children may have their autistic behaviour masked by additional, associated problems arising from sensory or cognitive impairment. Parents of these children may well just be told that their child is developmentally delayed. The statement of the child's special education needs is likely to refer to severe learning difficulties and the need for small group teaching and a structured curriculum. Provision is liable to be made in a school for children with severe learning difficulties. Autism is only likely to be raised as an issue if parents or concerned teachers feel the child's needs are not being met or if the child comes into contact with a knowledgeable professional.

The aim of the 1981 Education Act was that a child's educational needs should be identified and met through individual assessment rather than through association with a 'label' or category of need. In practice, because the fine ideal behind this aim has been mediated through pressures of time and finance, many statements of special educational need are reduced to bland generalities which simply relate to new categories such as 'severe learning difficulties'. Many statements of provision are merely re-statements of the local education authority provision already available.

If the authority does not make special provision for children with autism, there may well be resistance to statements suggesting placement in a school 'catering for the needs of autistic children'. This can be seen as an attempt to dictate the actual school, rather than specify the type of provision. Attempts to relate provision more specifically to the needs of the child may founder on the amount of detail required or on the uncertainty in predicting developmental patterns in autism. There is as yet no agreed suitable or appropriate curriculum, or even mode of curriculum delivery, that would permit short-hand statements such as 'a curriculum adapted to meet the needs of an autistic child' to be made.

Realistically, there is unlikely to be specialist provision available in every authority to meet the needs of all children who are autistic. It is not even certain that specialist provision will always be the preferred option; children who are mildly autistic or who are intellectually able may well have more to gain from an integrated setting, providing their special needs are recognized and accommodated. Even less able children may benefit from being alongside more sociable children with other learning difficulties providing, once again, that informed and explicit teaching methods enable them to benefit.

Sadly, many autistic children with severe learning difficulties are in settings where their needs are not understood and where they pose considerable management problems for the classroom teacher. In such situations, the child may be 'contained' within a school rather than educated, or the child may demand so much of the teacher's time and energy that the education of the other children in the class is put at risk. Sometimes the appropriate response would be to increase the understanding and thus the effectiveness of the teacher; sometimes the best solution would be to transfer the child to specialist provision.

EDUCATIONAL MANAGEMENT

The management of the child with autism in an educational setting will vary according to the nature of that setting. Clearly, different issues are involved in managing a class of children who are autistic than in managing a class where there is only one child with autism.

Whatever the setting, the different behaviours exhibited by different children with autism, taken with their varying educational needs, will also have a considerable influence on management strategies. There is a consensus in informed circles (based on research findings and considerable practical experience) that children with autism benefit most from structured educational settings rather than those where a more psychodynamic or 'acting out' approach is adopted.

The first management task for the teacher then is to establish this structure. In as much as it is possible to generalize at all about children with autism, it can be said that they both resist doing anything new and that they like to do what they are used to doing. The corollary of this is that, whereas the major battle will be first getting the child to accept the discipline of sitting to work, once the routine has been established, this problem disappears. Visitors to a specialist school will often express surprise to see a child they had seen running riot in another setting only a few weeks previously, now seemingly happily sitting at a table engaged in some table-top activity.

Some visitors express dismay to see young children sitting and working in this 'formal' way when they feel they should be exploring their environment, actively engaged in their own learning. It has to be pointed out that few children who are autistic are able to benefit from undirected activity. The first educational priority is to get them into a situation where they are able to concentrate on the task in hand and not being continually distracted by their fears or obsessions. This is only the beginning, of course – it then becomes important to ensure that they are engaged in educationally worthwhile activities. It is this initial step, however, that represents the key management task when a child with autism first enters school. Once the behaviour is under control, it may then be possible (and indeed desirable) to teach children ways of exploring the environment in a productive manner and becoming less passive or dependent in their learning.

This initial management task is made easier if children are young enough to be physically maintained in their seats while being rewarded for staying there. But, when all their uninhibited energy is directed at escape, even a six year old can be fearsomely strong. There is also an ethical issue involved with any form of restraint, sometimes even a legal one. Certainly, many teachers feel uncomfortable if they are required constantly to battle physically with a child. A preferable strategy, therefore, would be first to entice the child into the seat, then reward him or her for progressively longer time spent sitting at the table engaged on an activity. To begin with, mere approach to the table can bring the reward but then, in gradual steps, the time before gaining the reward is lengthened until the condition of being engaged in work is introduced.

The success of any such strategy depends on finding a suitable reward, defining a reward as anything that, presented immediately consequent on a behaviour, increases the likelihood of that behaviour recurring. This means that a reward is only a reward if it works! So different things will act as rewards for different children.

Children who are autistic may not like the things children are expected to like, or at least they may not like them well enough for them to act as a reward. Very few children, for example, understand or appreciate praise. Telling a child with autism he is a 'good boy' may have very little effect on his behaviour and hugging or putting an arm round a child may even act as a punishment! On the other hand, many children who are autistic have possessions or activities to which they are passionately attached. These can be made to work as powerful reinforcers for acceptable behaviour.

Rewards do not always have to be sweets: unexpected foodstuffs can have idiosyncratic reward value. There was the child who would work for a spoonful of piccalilli or a piece of raw onion! Music, too, can be a powerful reward, as can the opportunity to play on a swing or flick through the pages of a catalogue. As we have seen, children who are autistic come to enjoy the activities they are used to doing. Thus it may even become possible to arrange a child's timetable so that one activity is used to reinforce another. The day starts with the new, or least acceptable, activity and successful completion of that activity (or the section of it that forms the target for the day) allows the child to go on to a more favoured activity. Of course, timetabling constraints limit access to the swimming pool, the hall, or the mini-bus, making this approach impossible for some activities but it can be a useful approach to take for individual tasks within a particular session.

The approach of rewarding acceptable behaviour can be applied across different settings. Its success in developing compliant behaviour is really only limited by the ability to find suitable and effective rewards. Yet even these may not be sufficient by themselves to remove, or even reduce, all unwanted behaviour. If, however, a rewarded behaviour can be found which is incompatible with the behaviour you want to eliminate or discourage then, provided the reward is powerful enough, it may be used to replace the undesirable behaviour. I once managed to eliminate masturbation in the classroom by getting the child concerned to play a piano. Because he found piano playing intrinsically rewarding, at first it was sufficient simply to give him access to the piano. (Care needs to be taken when instituting such a programme that the rewarding activity is not offered as soon as the child engages in the unwanted activity – the 'distraction' approach – or it will simply serve to reinforce that unwanted behaviour.) What I had to do in this case was to identify the conditions under which the masturbation occurred (in the classroom, usually during any work period), then introduce the rewarding activity into that situation before the unwanted behaviour had an opportunity to start. Unfortunately, it was not possible in this school to move the large piano into the classroom, nor was the small electric organ, tried as a substitute, effective in competing with the masturbation. So I adopted an alternative strategy of physically prompting a very simple task before the child could begin to masturbate and then quickly whisking the child out to the piano as a reward for engaging in that activity. After a week's intensive training the work activity was being carried out without prompting and we were able gradually to increase the periods when the child would work at this and similar tasks before getting his reward of a session on the piano.

Obsessive behaviour

The last example should not be taken to imply that masturbation is necessarily an undesirable act. Very few behaviours are in themselves completely undesirable (with the possible exception of aggressive or self-mutilating behaviours); they may simply be inappropriate in that setting. Or they may become so self-absorbing as almost completely to preoccupy the child, leaving little time for more productive educational activities. A feature of the obsessive behaviour of children with autism is that it is rarely self-limiting. They never seem to have 'enough' of, or be satisfied by the favoured activity. So allowing them free rein in the hope they will become bored or satiated is seldom an effective strategy. At some point, if any productive learning is to occur, the teacher will need to intervene. And it is usually better to intervene as early as possible in the development of an obsession.

This raises the question of whether children who are autistic should be prevented from indulging in their particular obsession at all times – including 'free time' – be it at school, at home, or in the residential setting. My earlier proposition that practice only serves to reinforce the obsession would suggest a draconian approach would be best. Yet even the best theoretical decisions have to be tempered by pragmatism and by humanity. At a practical level, it is seldom possible for teachers, parents or care-staff to monitor each child's activities 24 h a day. It is better that children learn where and when the behaviour will be tolerated rather than learn they can sometimes 'get away' with the behaviour when no-one is watching. At a humane level, many children with autism appear to derive comfort – if not pleasure – from their obsessions, and it would seem unnecessarily cruel to deprive them of this without good reason. In the classroom, a good case can be made for attempting to remove the obsessive behaviour so as to allow more beneficial skills to be acquired. The same, however, cannot be argued for situations where the child is not being engaged in active learning. In those cases, a decision to eliminate or prevent the behaviour would have to be based on the intrinsic harm the behaviour represented either to the individual or to other people.

It should not be forgotten that we all have behaviours that we would not necessarily indulge in at work, or even in public, but which are perfectly acceptable in the privacy of our own homes. As children who are autistic seldom get granted the privilege of privacy, we should be careful not to burden them with abnormal and unnecessary constraints.

Aggression and self-injurious behaviour

Behaviour that falls within these two categories can be so distressing, and its handling so time-consuming for teachers, parents and care staff, that management of such behaviour merits a section to itself.

It might be prudent to begin by stressing that there are no easy answers. Decisions on a suitable strategy can only be made in the light of detailed knowledge of both child and situation in which the behaviour occurs. These strategies need to be monitored closely and adapted or changed if they are not working. And there will be some children, alas, whose problems appear intractable. Nevertheless these serious problems need to be tackled, if only for the reason that we cannot ignore them. In doing so, there are some general issues to be considered and some general points to be made.

First, we need to define the terms we are using or, at least, decide which behaviours we consider fall into these categories. The term 'aggressive' is not a simple, objective label for a well-defined category of behaviour; it involves an interpretation of that behaviour. We may witness a child hit another child or we may ourselves be the victim of a painful bite. It might seem reasonable to conclude that these are instances of aggressive behaviour. But, if we look at the situation from the child's point of view, a different picture may emerge. If a child with autism is feeling threatened by another child (and the 'threat' might only be that the other child is standing too close for comfort), that child may have no way of communicating his or her feeling of being threatened, or of asking the other child to go away. This 'hit' might then be seen as a communicative act. Of course, the child who has autism may not be aware of the communicative function involved in the act. He or she may simply have developed an effective strategy for being left alone . . . you hit out and people go away. But if we accept that what is intended is a form of communication rather than just an unpleasant act that needs to be eliminated, then our teaching approach will reflect this recognition. We will still want to eliminate the hitting, but will now appreciate that we are far more likely to be successful if we simultaneously teach children a more acceptable way of communicating the fact that they want to be left alone.

By considering the circumstances leading to the bite, we may also find that alternative views of the behaviour lead to different approaches in dealing with it. A common trigger for such apparently 'aggressive' behaviour in children who are autistic is pressure to work either at something new or something they find difficult. Or perhaps their initial attempts at performing the task have failed.

An equally common trigger is being prevented from engaging in some obsessive activity. In the latter case, the frustration underlying the behaviour is obvious. What we need to give the child is hope – some understanding that the behaviour is not being prevented forever. At some point (which should be clearly identified), the child will be allowed to engage in that activity once more. The problems lie first in identifying for the child the periods during which the behaviour will be permitted, when the child may have no, or very little, understanding of language, then in enabling the child to wait for those periods. Because many children with autism have great difficulty in waiting in any situation, this is a skill that needs to be taught. Periods of waiting (very short at first – perhaps just 30 seconds to start with) should be introduced into different situations. Children are given some words both to associate with waiting and with the ultimate satisfaction of gaining what they want. Suitable words might be 'coming' or 'soon'.

Where the child's 'aggression' seems to be a response to task difficulty, it might be helpful to regard it as communicating just that. Our response then is partly to reassure but also to teach the child more effective strategies both to cope with the task and to ask for help. Alternatively, we may need either to adjust the level of difficulty of the task or the mode of presentation. Of course, because we do not want to reinforce the biting, or any other form of aggressive behaviour, we should not allow children to escape from the task as a consequence of biting (although it can be difficult to persist while you are still in pain or shock). We should aim physically to prompt children to continue with the task for at least a brief period, then teach them to signal (by prompted word or sign) that they want us to leave, at which point we can go to lick our wounds and reconsider our future teaching approaches.

The point of this lengthy preamble is not to deny that some behaviour needs eliminating but to recognize that the label 'aggressive' neither helps us understand why it arises nor suggests ways that might be effective in bringing about its elimination. If, for example, analysis of the situation suggests the behaviour can best be seen as a means of communication, then that immediately suggests alternative strategies we might teach the child to get the message across. 'Aggression' somehow suggests we are talking about a characteristic of the child. Then we start to look for factors within the child that might be responsible for the aggression and – while such factors may well exist – there is little we can do to alter them. At the same time we may be neglecting factors within the situation itself which contributed to the aggression. These we can often do something about.

Self-injurious behaviour can be an even more disturbing pheno-menon, although at least other children are not in danger. There has been some research into the causes and motivation for the behaviour but, since each case may be different, those involved still need to analyse the particular circumstances for themselves. Some children seem to go through phases of such behaviour which cannot clearly be related to any external events. It may well be that – in those cases at least – the behaviour is triggered by factors within the child.

Sometimes, drug treatment is suggested. This may indeed be useful but children with autism have a tendency to react paradoxically to some drugs, so that 'tranquillizers' may be far from tranquillizing in their effect. And, most powerful drugs have significant side-effects. In any case, we should prefer not to have to resort to a 'chemical straightjacket' any more than an ordinary one. So, a method of choice would be first to seek to determine the cause for the behaviour then to use behavioural management techniques to deal with it.

There has been some suggestion that self-mutilation may trigger the release of brain chemicals which induce a state of euphoria; this not only renders children unaware of any pain engendered by the mutilation but also leads them to become addicted to the effects produced by these chemicals. Attempts have been made to reduce self-mutilation by getting children with autism to engage in activities that similarly release these chemicals, such as vigorous and sustained jogging. Some researchers have reported success with this method but my own attempt with a self-injuring child ended in failure. I could never get him to jog at sufficient speed or for long enough, although he was more than happy to watch me exhaust myself as I tried to encourage him to run. And self-mutilating children are clearly not always, or even not often, in a state of euphoria. The distress and unhappiness of such children can often be harder to witness than the injury itself, especially for parents.

Many children will attempt some form of self-restraint by wanting their hands tied, or keeping them trapped inside clothing. Once the restraint is removed, they tend immediately to start banging their faces, picking a wound, or carrying out whatever their particular form of self-mutilation is. I have known children attempt to eat meals with their hands emerging for brief moments from the neckline of the jumper inside which they are encased. Under such circumstances it can be tempting to leave children 'tied up', or with the sleeves of their jumper pulled over their hands, if this is what gives them security. There are two difficulties with this approach. Hands that are encased in clothing or otherwise restricted cannot be used to engage in fruitful occupation so that children's educational opportunities are liable to be very limited. Then, as with other obsessive behaviours, this behaviour is not self-limiting, nor are children happy to stay at one level of restraint. Thus, whilst having their hands up their sleeves may be enough at first to prevent the distressing behaviour, soon children will also require gloves or to hold their hands inside their jumpers and so on. Eventually, whatever restraints are imposed seem insufficient and we are forced to intervene.

Attempts have also been made to deal with the problems at a physical level. This is seldom successful either. One child had made the inside of his cheek sore by continually biting and gnawing at it. Doctors decided to deal with this by removing some of his molar teeth so that his remaining teeth could not normally come into contact with his cheek. But they could be helped to make contact if the cheek was pushed in from the outside with a finger and this was what the boy did. Removal of the teeth had been completely ineffective in eliminating the behaviour.

Unfortunately, there seems to be no short cut which pre-empts careful observation of the context for the behaviour so that strategies based on analysis of these observations can be devised. This is not to say that behavioural strategies, such as those suggested for eliminating other unwanted behaviour, will always work but they do seem to be the best we have.

ASSESSMENT FOR EDUCATION

It used to be common folklore that children with autism are impossible to assess; certainly there are persistent difficulties. However, as expertise has developed, it has been shown that children who are autistic can be assessed as reliably as other children. The assessor does, however, need to be aware of the potential problems in both performing the assessment and interpreting the results.

The initial problem with children who are hyperactive and autistic is to get them to come and stay 'on-task' long enough for an assessment to take place. Any problems of working with a 'strange' person will tend to be less significant for children with autism who are liable to go off as happily with a stranger as with their teacher, or even their parents. Even so, the results are likely to be more valid if the assessing is done by people who know the individual child and have already established some control over the child's behaviour.

Whereas the results of many standardized tests are invalid if children are rewarded for their performance (this would constitute training), as long as you do not reward actual responses there is nothing to stop you rewarding the child for sitting at the table and attending to the task. Some criterion-referenced tests (tests that relate a child's performance to a criterion behaviour rather than comparing the child to others, as is the case with norm-referenced tests like IQ tests or standardized reading tests) allow a period of pre-test training to give the child the idea of what is required, so ensuring optimum performance on the test. There is no reason why the child cannot be rewarded during this pre-test training, provided all the responses are not rewarded so that the child becomes disappointed and ceases to respond during the test proper.

Another major problem in assessing children with autism lies in their difficulties in understanding language. Where these difficulties are severe, it is best to choose tests that do not rely on language for their administration. There are performance scales for most IQ tests, and there are IQ tests that have been specifically designed for children with communication problems (usually for deaf children). The skilled teacher can usually find ways of presenting curriculum-based tests or tests of developmental level in a non-verbal way, unless of course it is language ability that is being assessed.

More problems arise when the child's language difficulties are not so obvious. For example, a child who is autistic may fail to score on a test when the instruction that needs to be followed to demonstrate understanding is 'show me!' This is a common feature of many tests. However, it involves the word 'show', which derives its meaning from an understanding of interpersonal relationships, a significant area of confusion for most children with autism. Faced with the instruction to 'show me x!', children who are autistic may demonstrate their lack of comprehension by simply echoing the phrase, by failing to comply with the instruction or by becoming increasingly agitated and aggressive. A test may conclude that the child does not understand any of the concepts (the x's) being tested whereas, if the instruction is couched in terms of some concrete action that the child understands (such as 'put your hand on!' or even 'touch!' x) rather than 'show me', the child may well be able to comply.

Assessing language and communication

Tests of language ability itself may be equally misleading. Problems with understanding verbal instructions may underestimate the child's overall understanding, but understanding may equally well be over-estimated by the testing procedure. Most tests are based on the assumption that the artificial test situation, where the natural context cannot be used to give a clue to meaning, will prove more difficult for the child; thus the child who responds correctly in the test situation is assumed to have 'real-world' knowledge of the verbal concepts as well. This assumption cannot be made about children with autism. They may have learnt the correct responses to the test materials (especially if they have been tested before) but have no idea of how these relate to the language of everyday life.

Tests of expressive language, based on an analysis of spontaneous speech, may overestimate the child's grammatical ability unless care is taken to exclude all instances of delayed echolalia from the sample. Even articulation difficulties (admittedly not very common in children who are autistic) may be masked where the sample only includes echoed speech rather than the child's own creative productions. These might reflect a different level of phonetic ability altogether. As with understanding, expressive ability may be over-estimated if the child's production in a test situation, where the language may have been elicited or cued in some way, is taken as indicative of the child's ability in real life situations.

When assessing the linguistic ability of a child with autism, it is often even more important than for other children to assess the child's communicative ability. This can be done from naturalistic classroom or home-based observations although schedules, such as the Pre-Verbal Communication Schedule which was piloted on children with autism, help focus attention both on the many different ways in which the child may be communicating and on the range of pre-communicative behaviours which could be developed to fulfil a communicative function.

In the case of verbal children, it is not sufficient merely to itemize the vocabulary and grammatical structures children can use and understand. We also need to assess their ability to use those language forms to communicate and their ability to understand the communications of others. To make this assessment, we can use our observations of each child to check the number and type of communicative functions the child can use and understand; functions drawn from a list such as that included in the TEACCH programme (Treatment and Education of Autistic and Related Communication in Handicapped Children is a comprehensive service programme for people of all ages with autism and related developmental disorders, based in North Carolina, USA). We will also want to look at the child's ability to carry on conversations. For that we need to look at the discourse strategies the child can use. These strategies include such things as being able to initiate a conversation, take turns in a conversation by creating pauses and not interrupting others, comment on or extend the topic of the other person's discourse, or have appropriate strategies for changing the topic, paying attention to listener feedback and some way of rephrasing information the listener does not understand. There are now formats for assessing classroom discourse strategies.

Assessing other subjects

The problems in assessing performance in other curriculum areas will be similar to those already mentioned. Subjects like mathematics are particularly problematic since some children who are autistic will have good, even remarkable, computational ability but no understanding of mathematical concepts, especially when they are expressed linguistically. The problem becomes one of assessing the mathematical ability divorced from the linguistic restrictions. As with language, the tester should not let an ability to perform calculations mask the very real problems the child may have in applying mathematical skills to practical problem solving. It is in the social application of mathematical skill, such as shopping, or timing an event, or estimating the materials needed for a task, that the child's ability needs to be assessed. And, these are the areas where teaching is likely to need to be directed. Formal mathematical tests can give a very misleading impression of the child's abilities.

Similarly, reading tests may overestimate the ability of the 'hyperlexic' child with autism who somehow manages to read without understanding. It is important to assess the ability to follow written instructions or understand a written news event rather than assign the child some spurious 'reading age' from a standardized assessment.

THE CURRICULUM FOR CHILDREN WITH AUTISM

As indicated above, there is no agreed, suitable curriculum for children who are autistic. Certainly the content will depend, to some extent, on the age and ability of the child as well as the precise nature of the autistic difficulties. The educational needs of an able 12 year old are going to differ from those of a six year old with severe learning difficulties, even if they are both autistic.

However, there are some substantive areas that need to be part of the taught curriculum for children with autism, which form only part of the 'hidden' curriculum for other children – if they feature at all. There are also teaching approaches and ways of delivering the curriculum that apply particularly, if not exclusively, to children with autism.

Before looking at these areas, however, when devising a curriculum for children with special needs, there is an issue of fundamental concern to be addressed: whether its purpose should be remedial or compensatory. A remedial curriculum would look at the central difficulties imposed by autism and try to devise content areas that would help children overcome those difficulties. For children with autism, such an approach would be exemplified by strategies aimed at getting children to overcome their social/cognitive, behavioural and communication problems by trying to teach them to gain these skills in the way they are normally acquired. The aim would be eventually for children to be functioning normally, although still perhaps to be delayed in certain areas. In other words, the problems would have been 'remedied'.

A compensatory approach, on the other hand, does not attempt to produce normal functioning but seeks to give children compensatory skills or techniques which will enable them to function in the same way as other children, but by abnormal means. The classic example of a compensatory device is a pair of spectacles which does nothing to improve the actual visual capacity of the person's eyes, but does correct for the defect. The person is thereby enabled to have normal vision albeit through a technical device. An example of a compensatory curricular device for children who are mute and autistic would be to teach them a sign language which would help compensate for (though by no means resolve) some of their communication problems, but would not teach them to communicate in the way other children do.

This issue will come up again, but it is my view that both approaches are required when devising a curriculum for children with autism. We need to tackle some of their fundamental problems in the hope that we can find a way of remedying them, but we also need to give these children some compensatory strategies for getting by in the confusing world in which they must learn to function as independently as possible.

LANGUAGE AND COMMUNICATION

Perhaps the most obvious and persistent of difficulties experienced by children who are autistic is that of communication. As we have seen in earlier chapters, a significant proportion of children with autism will remain mute or have very little language that is used communicatively. There is a dramatic drop in the chances that a child will ever talk if the first word has not been uttered by six years and, again, a poor chance of ever speaking in phrases if such speech does not follow the production of the first words within six years. The chances of learning to speak after the age of 13 years are almost nil.

However, even those children who do have very good, syntactically correct speech will still suffer from communication difficulties. By the same token, teaching the child who is mute and autistic to use signs will not in itself solve the child's difficulties in understanding how to communicate with those signs. In order to communicate, a child needs something to communicate about, something to communicate for, and something to communicate with. Some children with autism, like other children with severe language difficulties, or sensory problems or specific language difficulties, will need help and specific teaching to meet all those requirements. But, given that these three pre-conditions for communication exist, then almost all other children will communicate; only children who are autistic need specific teaching in what communication is for.

Language programmes, whether of spoken language or sign, concentrate on giving the child some means both of communicating and of understanding the language of others. For children who are autistic, understanding the language (in terms of understanding the literal meaning of the words or signs and their combination into phrases or sentences) is only the first step in understanding communication. They need to understand that when mummy says 'why don't you take your bicycle outside, darling and play in the garden?' the syntax and semantics may suggest this is a question to which the child should reply, giving reasons for playing indoors with the bicycle. But, in a communicative sense, this is a command. Very young, pre-school children have been shown to be capable of making this distinction in meaning; they understand the communicative intent of messages because they understand the social context. This implies that they are able to look beyond the literal meaning of the words and phrases and to use their understanding of people's motives to work out what was intended. Children with autism have been shown to have particular difficulty imputing motives to others, and so in understanding the intentions behind messages.

To the extent that language programmes teach language out of social context, they do nothing to address this central problem and so are to be avoided with children who are autistic. The priority must be to teach the child to communicate, however much – for obvious reasons – we should like the child to communicate in as sophisticated and normal a manner as possible. The more the method of communication mirrors that of the community, the more people will understand the child and the more socially acceptable he or she will be. The child also needs as sophisticated a language system as he or she can manage to use as a tool in thinking and problem solving.

The TEACCH programme has developed a communication programme specially geared to the needs of children who are autistic. Many teachers would want to adapt aspects of the programme towards a more interactive, less behaviouristic teaching style. The strength of the programme, however, is that it includes the specific teaching of communication functions as well as teaching the meaning of the language and language structure. It also stresses the different natural contexts in which the language is to occur and the importance of teaching children to generalize the language they have learnt from one situation or context to another. I have bitter experience of the folly of teaching language skills to children with autism in separate, one-to-one sessions only to find that these skills (so rewardingly 'easy' to teach in such sessions) failed to be used or understood out of that context. There may be a value in using these individual sessions for some initial work with a child, particularly related to some aspects of assessment, but communication skills cannot be taught or understood out of the communicative context.

A further feature of the TEACCH programme to serve as a useful reminder to those working with children who are autistic, is its insistence that a child must not be expected to learn more than one thing at a time. Thus, if a child is to be taught a new vocabulary item (a new word or sign) then he or she should not be expected to use it in a new semantic category. For example, the child could learn the word or sign for 'apple' as a food, because he or she already understands the semantic category of food and knows the names of other foods. But the child should not be expected to understand 'apple' as a fruit in a botanical sense (as a fleshy part of a plant, surrounding the seeds) or even as a sub-category of food (compared to vegetables or meat, say) until the word or sign has been learnt. Nor should the child be expected to use 'apple' outside the context where he or she is already communicating (home and classroom perhaps, or only one of those), or for any different communicative purpose than already established (most probably this will mean learning to use 'apple' as a request for an apple, since the request function is the one most readily used and understood by children with autism).

Language as a teaching medium

This focus on communication has other implications for the way we teach and use language, in school in particular. It affects what we decide to teach in terms of vocabulary, and the syntactic forms chosen. If our aim is to teach children what communication is for, and help them use their language for communicative purposes, then we should select a vocabulary and syntax that reflects what they want to communicate about and will give them a way of doing it. There is little point in teaching any set vocabulary of words or signs (as some 'language' programmes suggest you do) or in teaching statements before questions just because they appear first in developmental terms, if a child is going to want to make a request, using the question form.

Although many programmes or kits have some useful features which can be taken out and adapted to meet the needs of children with autism, they should always be used critically rather than slavishly, judging them against the criterion of how well they meet the communicative needs of a particular child. Some programmes teach a peculiar language style that is more suited to written than spoken language, apparently under the misapprehension that it is more 'correct'. Thus, you are told that when you show a picture of a bird in a tree and ask 'where is the bird?', you must not accept as 'correct' a child pointing to the bird (although this clearly demonstrates that the child has not only understood the question, but also understands the communicative context in which both of you can see the picture and where the child is pointing), nor even a child saying 'there!' (accompanied by a pointing gesture) or 'in the tree' (although this demonstrates understanding of elipsis where the subject and verb are 'understood' by reference to an earlier utterance). Instead, you are meant to wait for, or prompt, the child to say 'the bird is in the tree'. This is precisely the kind of abnormally pedantic utterance we find all too often in the speech of children who are autistic, where the communicative context (which makes this level of specificity in language inappropriate) has not been understood.

By the same token, we should examine the language style we routinely use in school to see how appropriate it is for children who are having problems understanding what communication is all about. It has been shown that when normally developing children whose parents have not adopted a 'teaching' style in talking to them (as many predominantly middle-class parents do) come into school, they are at first completely bewildered by the unusual and strange forms of communication they find there. They take time to adjust and can be put at an educational disadvantage if the teacher is not sensitive to these difficulties. But most children do eventually come to understand the 'educational style'. They learn that, unlike at home, the teacher is not interested in topics the child has initiated but wants the child to talk about teacher-chosen topics. Unlike normal conversation, you do not contribute to a discussion when there is something you want to say. You may have to put up your hand before being allowed to speak, or you may be directed to speak when you have nothing to say (and may positively not want to speak).

And then the teacher does not use questions (as their pre-school experience has led children to expect they should be used) to ask for information or even to make requests. The teacher perpetually asks questions to which she clearly already knows the answer. 'What's my name?' she asks the class, a question which could only be understood under normal conversational conventions if she was suffering from some form of amnesia. 'What's the time?' she asks as she holds up a large clock on which the time is clearly displayed. Are the children meant to conclude that she does not know how to tell the time and is asking for their assistance? Hardly. After a while in school they come to understand that these are not 'real' questions at all but 'display questions'. What the teacher is asking is not 'what is this?', but 'do you know what this is?' 'Can you tell me what this is?' Display your knowledge so I can find out if you know.

As we have seen, normally developing children have problems coming to terms with these new uses of language (which are peculiar to the educational context). Children with severe learning difficulties also find this novel usage a problem. It is only to be expected then that it will present a serious difficulty for children with autism, who have problems understanding any conversational conventions, let alone contradictory ones. Given that the task of teaching communication skills is difficult and time-consuming, I would question the value of teaching the child a set of conventions and rules of use only within the educational context. They would certainly mark you off as bizarre if you tried to use them with your friends, or in the pub!

This difficulty in understanding the educational conventions of language usage is not, as we have seen, peculiar to children who are autistic, although it may be particularly severe for them. There are, however, some aspects of understanding language that are uniquely related to the specific features of autism. At least some children with autism do not appear to learn or acquire language through the normal process of building up from single words to two-word phrases to longer phrases and sentences. Instead their language develops from full echoed phrases which are then broken down and the parts recombined to create new meanings. Thus a child may begin by echoing 'do you want a biscuit?' as a request when he or she wants a biscuit. This may be bizarre semantically in that the child fails to change either the pronoun appropriately or the question form into a statement, but it is recognizable as a communicative request. The child may then start to use it to request other items by changing one word as, for example, 'do you want a sweet?'. Other language forms may develop in similar ways. The breaking-down process may not always be complete so some words remain forever 'stuck together'. One child could never refer to a 'television' as such, but always called it a 'watch television', and she always referred to herself as 'me please', having been taught to use the correct pronoun instead of her name when answering the question, 'who wants a drink?'. Similarly, long after she understood about gender, she could not say 'good boy' since 'good' was associated with 'girl' addressed to herself, so she had to say 'good girl boy' instead.

If children who are autistic try to understand language, and to remember it as specific speech 'events', they may well not understand it can refer to contexts outside the one in which the language originally occurred. This has a double effect. On the one hand, contexts may trigger speech memories in a child so that when some crucial aspect of the original context is repeated, the child may be prompted to produce some phrase originally heard in that context, in effect producing 'delayed echolalia'. An example of this was given by Kanner. One child used 'the damned potatoes are burning' as a request for food when the expression, first heard when feeling hungry and watching lunch being prepared, was triggered by those same feelings of hunger. I knew a child who always exclaimed, 'don't spit, Janey!' whenever anyone was cross with her, regardless of the cause, because she associated being told off with that phrase.

The other effect of seeing language as divorced from its real-life reference is that a child may look for set answers to set questions. The child will apply this to his or her own situation being reluctant to accept, 'go on then!' as permission to go out to play, but persisting in the request, 'can't I go out to play?' until told, 'Yes, you can', as he or she was the first time. Children will also apply the formula approach to questions asked by the teacher. If you have no idea that the days of the week refer to the passages of time, it can be very frustrating to have the answer, 'Monday', you learnt so laboriously to the question, 'What day is it today?', rejected on Tuesday! In respect of the weather, one boy I knew dealt with this problem by always answering 'cloudy' to the question 'What's the weather like today?' He had learnt that (given it was the UK), this was nearly always right!

The way to deal with problems like this is to avoid using the question format and use an incomplete phrase such as, 'the weather today is . . .' and then whisk the child out to consult the weather before replying. In that way, the child gets the idea that the language relates to actual experience, learning to examine the weather before making a response.

Teachers often become frustrated trying to teach children with autism colour names, and despair when a colour the child seemed to know perfectly well one day is forgotten the next. What is often overlooked is that a child may indeed know his or her colours but you may only find this out if you discover a way of asking about colour that makes sense to the child. If a child sees you hide a sweet in one of several, differently coloured but otherwise identical boxes, and is then asked to tell you where it is, he or she may well be able to name the colour correctly. Yet the same child, faced with the same box and asked, 'What colour is this?' may, regardless of the actual colour of the box, try to remember the last correct answer he or she gave to that question. The child may simply not realize that 'real world facts' such as the actual colour of objects has anything to do with the question.

The importance of ensuring that the language makes sense to the child affects all communication in the classroom. The limitations of a strictly behavioural approach to language teaching have been recognized for other children with severe learning difficulties, yet it has been suggested that children with autism may still need this highly structured, teacher-directed approach. It seems to me that a child who does not understand what language is for, or how it can be used to communicate, is least able to benefit from an approach that divorces language from its meaningful context. Children with autism already try to remember language as a series of meaningless statements. This tendency will only be reinforced if language is taught in this way. It is not surprising these children then fail to generalize or go on to use the language they have learnt outside language sessions. The need is to teach language in the context of its use, so the child is taught to request food at lunch-time, when it is appropriate, and is not given food as a reward for a totally unrelated language statement.

Teachers are sometimes dismayed to think they will not be able to use the few powerful rewards the child will work for to reinforce language use. In fact, it is possible to continue to use these rewards, but the approach has to be more subtle. If the child is only interested in sweets, then these can be used, but not simply as a reward for an unrelated activity. As in the example above, a sweet can be hidden to get the child to name colours or perhaps the objects on which they are placed. This may not be a natural situation for obtaining sweets but it is an understandable 'game' context, and naming the colour, or whatever else, does have a proper communicative function. The child is telling the teacher where to find the sweet, and being given the sweet you have found is really quite a natural consequence of the action: it makes a lot more sense than just being given a sweet for naming something.

Interpersonal skills

Apart from communication, the other main area of the curriculum that has to be specially designed to meet the needs of children with autism is that related to the teaching of interpersonal skills. There are other groups of children for whom this is a priority (children with emotional and behavioural difficulties, for example) but, for them, it is usually either a matter of re-adjusting faulty strategies, or giving them greater awareness of and control over the strategies they are using. By contrast, children who are autistic are likely to need to learn interpersonal skills 'from scratch'. They need help in tolerating and understanding the social behaviour of others, especially as it relates directly to them.

At the most basic level, they need to become aware of themselves as individuals and of others as distinct from themselves. This will involve playing touching and interactive games, similar to those played with a young baby. The wording and form of tickling or rough and tumble play that often signals the climax of such games can always be adjusted to suit the age and dignity of the child. First you perform the routine on the child's body, but once he or she is showing anticipation of this climax, you can switch to prompting the child to perform the actions on your body, while you go through the same routine. Once children have learnt to differentiate those situations where the actions are directed at them from those where they are directed at you, they have made some progress in acknowledging your existence.

Reciprocal games such as pat-a-cake will need to be taught by prompting children to turn their hands outwards towards yours. Most children with autism will try to copy the actions directly as they perceive them, that is they will attempt to 'pat' with their palms directed towards their own bodies. Mirror games in which you sit alongside the child, facing a mirror, and put make-up first on part of your face and then on the child's, or put a hat first on you and then on the child, also help to focus his or her attention on you and establish you as a distinct person.

Teaching children who are autistic both to pay attention to people and to establish joint attention to the environment with those around them is the first, essential step in establishing a shared frame of reference upon which understanding of language depends. This is far more than merely teaching them to make eye contact, a pointless action unless a child understands how eye contact is used to initiate and maintain communication. Of far greater importance is getting children with autism to see people as playing a significant part in meeting their needs. They need to be taught to seek attention or indicate the wish to communicate (even if, as is so often the case, it is only that they want something). Even children with a fair command of spoken language may need to be shown how to use eye-contact (with or without vocatives) to gain attention. You can use games in which the child being looked at is allowed to follow the instruction to do something desirable (such as, 'you can go and get a sweet!'), to help teach this. It is amazing how quickly some children learn to seek eye-contact during such games, when they can see the relevance of doing so!

Initially, joint attention can be taught by following the child's focus of interest and commenting on that. This is a way of ensuring the child is attending to the same item or event as you. If, as may very well be the case, the focus of the child's attention is his or her obsessional activity, your interference may well be resented and the child will either seek to exclude you or, failing that, abandon the activity. That is a pity in as much as you will not be able to use that particular activity during the session again, but you will still know that your intervention was noticed. The joint focus of attention will have been achieved, if only briefly.

Once you have managed to establish a joint focus of attention in this way on a number of occasions, you need to move on to the more difficult task of getting the child to focus on something that you have drawn to his or her attention. Again, you may have to start by using the child's interest to attract his or her attention. This may involve spinning the object you want to label (if the child's obsession is with spinning items) or draping it with Christmas tree lights, or hiding some favourite possession behind it, anything that will entice the child to look at whatever it is you are directing him or her to look at.

The final way of attaining a joint focus of attention is to comment on and label (often best done by using singing or rhythmic language) joint activities. These might be self-help routines, like washing hands or bathing, which occur on a regular basis. The child can then learn to identify a familiar sequence of actions with a familiar set of sung or spoken expressions.

Other difficulties in curriculum delivery

Apart from specific, substantive areas that will need explicit teaching, the way in which the curriculum for children with autism is delivered will also need adaptation to take account of their particular learning difficulties. We have already seen how the teacher will need to modify her use of language in the classroom. Most subjects are usually taught in a social context, using language to issue instructions, direct attention, explain concepts and consolidate learning. Poor understanding of language itself and of the social context for its use can cause problems in all these areas for the child who is autistic.

Where possible, instructions should be given by demonstration or even by actually manipulating the child through the actions required. Children with autism have been described as having 'tunnel attention'. Because there is only a limited range of stimuli that they will associate together, this may mean that verbal directions are simply not associated with the appropriate items or events. We may have to resort to some of the more 'unusual' ways of attracting attention mentioned above. In particular, even when they have developed a language, children with autism seem to have great difficulty in using language to aid thinking.

Children with autism have been credited with good memory skills and certainly their memory for events in their lives can be extraordinarily detailed and long-lasting. Paradoxically, it is this apparent 'strength' that is in fact a clue to the difficulties they have with memory. Children with autism have very good 'episodic' memories (compared to their general level of cognitive ability, of course) that is, they can remember in minute detail things they have seen and heard (and perhaps smelled and touched, but we are not sure about that). What they have difficulty in doing is remembering the 'gist' of events or the important features of something they have seen or heard. So their memories become 'clogged' with irrelevant details. They are not storing events or facts within a meaningful framework, neither are they making sense (almost literally) of their experiences. If they fail to store memories in a meaningful way, then these memories will not be readily accessible to voluntary control. Our memory for concepts and facts (our knowledge, in effect) provides us with mental models of how the world 'works'. When trying to remember the capital of France, we recall parts of what we know about France or capital cities; we do not (and probably could not) recall the exact circumstances when first we were told or discovered this fact. But if children with autism have difficulty in constructing these 'mental models', and store their memories as personal events, they will not necessarily be able to use them to help problem-solve. Instead, the memories will be triggered by environmental events that 'remind' the child of the previous experience.

Children who are autistic, therefore, will need training in recalling the salient points of experiences and relating them, in a meaningful way, to other experiences. Verbal children will need to be taught to re-tell events they have just witnessed, leaving out irrelevant detail. They will need practice in relating events one to another and classifying experiences meaningfully. Initially, this may be done by using pictures or symbols of some kind that single out these significant events or experiences which they can then learn to sequence and use in re-telling the story.

Computer-assisted learning

Some of the problems caused by the social and linguistic context of education can be solved with the use of computer-assisted learning. We need a remedial curriculum which helps children develop the social skills they lack, but we also need a compensatory curriculum that enables children to learn other strategies and to develop other cognitive skills without being handicapped by social and linguistic impairments.

The computer can provide both consistent stimulation and a patient, diagnostic teaching style that can be very helpful to the child who is autistic. It can be programmed to give prompts when one strategy fails so that the child does not react catastrophically to failure, as is characteristic of children with autism. The child seems to accept 'failure' on the computer as a machine simply 'not working' until he or she gets it right, whereas a teacher may be seen as 'responsible' for withholding a reward, and so become the focus of anger. Working with children who are autistic, often feels like engaging in battle. Succeeding in teaching the child something involves 'winning' in some way, with the inevitable corollary that the child has 'lost'. Computers can free both participants from the battle and help prevent passive reliance on the teacher which, again, is characteristic of children with autism. Good computer software (such as that found in Logo programs) will put children back in control of their own learning. There is the added advantage that many children with autism are fascinated by computers and so there is an intrinsic motivation to learn.

There remains the problem of seeing how far computer-taught skills transfer to other situations. I am currently engaged on work with a colleague to see whether a series of computer programs, shown to improve thinking skills in normally-developing young children, will be effective with children with autism, and whether any improvement will transfer to other problem-solving situations.

THE SOCIAL LIFE OF THE CHILD

Children who are autistic are often seen as intentionally withdrawing from social life, but, in reality, because they may have very little idea of how to relate to others, they may have little choice in the matter. Where a child is being educated in an integrated setting with more sociable children, the other children can be taught to help draw the child who has autism into their social world.

During the period between 6 and 12 years of age, it is often the case that children with autism will learn to interact socially, at some level, with those adults who have made the effort positively to intrude on their isolation. They almost never make spontaneous relationships with other children though (except perhaps brothers and sisters), partly because they do not know how to, partly because they are not motivated to, and partly because other children are often 'put off' by the bizarre behaviour and the social rebuffs of the child who is autistic. Other children need to be taught to overcome some of these barriers and to be positively encouraged to do so. They may not find the child with autism immediately satisfying as a playmate or friend, but even very young children can enjoy the experience of helping others (especially if this collaboration centres round some definite activity or task) and can gain much from it themselves. Children with autism will not benefit from the presence of other children simply by placing them among them, but they can get substantial benefit if the interactions are planned and purposeful.

Part of the school curriculum should be devoted to improving the social skills of children with autism in a way that will make them more socially acceptable, so making it easier for their families to include them in outings. Thus the timetable needs to include visits to shops, cafes, parks and playgrounds. They should be taught to wait in the sort of crowded conditions they are likely to experience in, for example, a doctor's surgery.

It may still be necessary to offer parents support and encouragement to teach the same skills at home, for it cannot be assumed that the child who is autistic will transfer behaviour from one situation to another. However, not only will it be easier to teach the behaviour if it has already been learnt at school, but parents will have the reassuring belief that it is possible to teach their child to wait quietly in a cafe to be served or to walk along the street holding someone's hand. It is seldom possible to offer solutions to problems, or teaching techniques that you can guarantee will work with all children. All it is possible to do is to say that this has been known to work with some children, and to offer that optimistic belief that is so necessary for the morale of those working with these difficult, but fascinating children.

FURTHER READING

AHTACA (1986) *The Special Curricular Needs of Autistic Children*, AHTACA, London.

Koegal, R.L., Rincover, A. and Egel, A.L. (eds) (1982) *Education and Understanding Autistic Children*, College Hill Press, San Diego

Schopler, E. and Mesibov, G.B. (eds) (1985) *Communication Problems in Autism*, Plenum Press, New York.

Schopler, E. and Mesibov, G.B. (eds) (1986) *Social Behaviour in Autism*, Plenum Press, New York.

Adolescence and early adulthood (1): The needs of the more able young adult

Gillian Taylor

It is beginning to be recognized that autism covers a very wide range of ability and disability. In its most severe form, autism is more readily identified but, as with disability of any kind, there must be a point where the dividing line between autism and 'normality' is blurred. The problems experienced by young people who are less handicapped may be less obvious but can nevertheless create severe difficulties for them.

The difficulties arise out of the same basic impairments which affect all people with the syndrome. The ability to relate to others and to the world around is distorted. People with autism do not perceive the links between other people's thoughts, feelings, ideas and their own; and language is not used as a tool for social inter-action. There is too a tendency towards obsessive interests which may inhibit contact with other people.

Such difficulties present major, persistent problems for more able young people with autism or people with Asperger's syndrome. As with classic autism, people described as having Asperger's syndrome (now, as indicated in Chapter 1, regarded less as a separate syndrome than as part of the spectrum of autistic conditions) engage in repetitive activities and show marked resistance to change. The obsessive quality of their interests can lead to an intense preoccupa-tion with particular subjects for which they may have a high level of skill.

The more obvious difficulties are associated with a lack of judge-ment and motivation which arises out of the obsessive personality. People with autism cannot weigh up the pros and cons of a situation. For instance, more able young people may have hobbies which, although acceptable interests within their peer group, are pursued to the exclusion of essential 'survival tasks', such as planning future events – be this the next meal or the next five years.

This chapter aims to look at the needs of this group of more able people with autism in adolescence and early adulthood. From my experience, they do need something over and above the educational and management programmes devised for other children with autism (although the tried and tested principles of intervention, structure, rules and routines, and pragmatic teaching methods still apply). The most important contribution towards the future success of this group of young people is the recognition that they will continue to need direct teaching of a wide range of life skills, including those which children who are not autistic acquire unthinkingly with increased life experience.

MAINSTREAM OR SPECIAL EDUCATION?

The educational significance of the problems faced by young people described as having Asperger's syndrome may be missed. In a mainstream school, they may be seen as eccentric and loners but, as long as their educational attainments remain within the normal range and their behaviour is not too disruptive, their presence will be tolerated. From my own experience, both in meeting young people with Asperger's syndrome and in working with more able children with autism (or those who have made good progress), it is arguable whether a mainstream education can provide for all their special educational needs.

Improvements in diagnosis have resulted in the recognition of more and more young people whose pattern of skills, handicaps and behaviour is regarded as fitting that of Asperger's syndrome. In general, these young people have not been diagnosed until their teenage years when attention has been drawn to their difficulties because they have not been able either to adapt their behaviour to a wider, less structured social context or cope with the larger expectations of adult life. Although, academic ability and behaviour permitting, they are likely to have coped at least for a time in local primary schools, some young people have emerged from schools for children with an emotional disturbance where their lack of understanding, inability to cope with change and resulting difficulties in behaviour have tended to be misunderstood and therefore inappropriately managed (and often exacerbated by the models around them). Some young people, not diagnosed until their teenage years, have been placed in schools for children with moderate learning difficulties, although, as the practice of integration becomes increasingly widespread, these schools are beginning to decline in number. Because such schools follow a secondary age curriculum, more in line with mainstream education, the adolescent with autism tends to fail.

There are also children with autism whose basic difficulties are masked because they possess both a facility for language and an awareness about the world around them. Again, the needs of these young people cannot readily be met within existing provision and it is concern for their future which may eventually lead to detailed assessment and a diagnosis of autism. Often young people who are undiagnosed until their teens have not had an education appropriate to their needs. They may have the language and learning skills to have acquired such factual information as has been explicitly taught, but the type of curriculum followed in mainstream schools, or in schools which aim to prepare a child for integration into ordinary schools, does not provide for young people who have difficulty in acquiring the sort of knowledge that one quite simply would not expect to have to teach. For even the most able of people with autism have difficulty in learning from peripheral experience. Whilst a rote-memory allows them to learn facts, systematic teaching of the broadest range of life skills is required if they are to live at all independently.

All young people who are autistic have difficulty in carrying out tasks requiring motivation, judgement and initiative. What causes more able young people most distress is an inability to comprehend the limits on their own freedom compared to the apparent licence others have to do as they please. It is not simply that they do not want to be autistic, but that they are totally unaware of the unseen rules which place restrictions on everyone's freedom of choice.

The number of young people who, although relatively verbal, able and aware of the world around them, are recognized as having difficulties which fall within the broad spectrum of autism, will increase as knowledge of the syndrome increases.

IMPLICATIONS FOR CURRICULUM PLANNING

The onset of puberty marks the beginning of a period of change where the child enters a developmental stage from which he or she will emerge an adult. Although this process may begin later for children who are autistic, they nonetheless show all the usual, physical signs of maturation.

Not only physiological changes are taking place though, it is a time when new social pressures are brought to bear on the young person. Childhood rules no longer apply and the young person's expectations, as well as those other people have of the young person, begin to alter. Young people who have not only the potential for greater independence but some awareness of what life has to offer, are rather more likely to experience the psychological impact of adolescence than young people who continue to require a high level of care and supervision.

Working, as we usually do, with the more handicapped child with autism, it is easy to forget the wide range of complex skills and information needed for everyday life by those capable of a more independent life-style. The more independence that is gained, the more complex and subtle the issues become. Limited social awareness, coupled with a lack of understanding that there are limitations on everyone's freedom to do as he or she pleases, can cause the adolescent and adult with autism much unhappiness. If any realistic level of independence is to be achieved, the need for the more able person with autism to be able to deal with life as it is outside the protection of a specialist service, is more important than any single academic skill.

Self-organization

Able people with autism do have skills and, much of the time, their use of language may be both sophisticated and appropriate. Academic skills can be developed to a high level, but they are of no help to people who have not yet learned to organize their lives. This is the area where able young people often fail: the need to get up on time, the need to be clean, the need to plan a day around essential events simply do not occur to them. Often, unless a very strict routine is established and maintained, the very people who make great strides academically are limited in their ability to perform those tasks associated with self-care or domestic life.

Although academic subjects are important if young people are to take their place in society, they cannot manage this without being given the tools for everyday survival. A university degree is not much use if you cannot meet your own domestic needs. This includes being able to set an alarm to get up at the right hour, judge the time it takes to wash, dress, shave, plan a budget, shop, prepare meals and eat, understand timetables, travel, manage money, ask appropriate questions and just be able to get on with other people in practical and socially meaningful ways.

Applying life skills

All these skills need to be taught in the appropriate context – in the right place at the right time. They are life skills which, unless explicit efforts are made to help make good the deficits in learning, no amount of formal teaching or 'traditional' education is going to provide. In promoting the more able child's greater potential for academic progress, it is easy to forget that judgement, organizational ability, an intuitive understanding of cause and effect – taken for granted in comparably able children who are not autistic – are missing.

It is relatively easy to sit academically able children with autism at a task in the classroom but they must be capable of using the learned skill in real life situations. Academic achievement does not mean that children will be able to transfer learning to the big outside world. What is the point of being able to calculate problems involving vast sums of money if you cannot manage road crossings, queue in a shop, ask rather than demand what you want, manoeuvre a trolley through a supermarket, or recognize that you need to go to a till where there is an assistant? Although the school where I worked had a very practical curriculum – tuck-shops and cafe were open each week to teach not just use of money but also appropriate behaviour in outside settings – a gap was discovered when a member of staff was out shopping at the same time as one of the senior pupils. It was a busy lunch-time and the member of staff thought that the pupil had found a cashpoint without a queue. She had, but neither was there a cashier!

Focusing on understanding

For able young people, rather than sticking to a mainstream school curriculum, it is important to unearth the gaps in learning and understanding. A very useful exercise, regularly conducted in a group of the most able young people at my school, was a weekly 'quiz'. Questions were related to everyday matters they had experienced, but which had possibly not been directly taught. For example:

'Where would you go to buy stamps?'
'Name three foods you could use to make a salad.'
'What do you need to wear if you are walking in a muddy field?'

By looking and talking about pictures, much can be gleaned about the deficits in children's learning and understanding of the commonplace meaning of events. It may not be easy to find suitable examples (as pictures whose message is implied rather than being explicit are required) but they can be useful for identifying some of those gaps. Take the example of a young man of 17 who had an excellent command of language and had been in mainstream education up to the age of 12. He could hold an interesting conversation and answer almost any question appropriately. When presented with a picture of two houses, one in good repair with curtains and a pretty garden, the neighbouring house with boarded-up windows, peeling paint and an unkempt garden, he indicated that the neat and tidy house was the empty one. His reason? 'The gate is closed.' Such responses show the idiosyncratic interpretation of events by people who are autistic – commonly ascribed meanings are not used to make sense of the world. We can only conclude that the more subtle information we each absorb unthinkingly from our environment is unavailable to them.

Such niceties of comprehension present the major impediment to independence in adulthood. People who do not understand the handicap have great difficulty in accommodating the literal way in which people with autism think. One 9-year old boy had such a remarkable command of language that visitors often asked why he needed to be at the school. He was able to run errands to the local shops for his parents and one day was sent with a carrier bag and money for some potatoes. He returned with the money and an empty carrier bag. When asked why he hadn't bought the potatoes he declared the shop assistant stupid as she had asked him if he wanted red or white whereas, 'everyone knows potatoes are brown'. Another young man, who could make single hot drinks, was just learning to make a selection. Sent off to the kitchen, he returned with one black coffee and another cup containing a mixture of milk and hot water. He had been asked for two coffees – one black, one white!

Any time spent in conversation with these young people, especially when simultaneously they are being confronted by a wide range of real life demands, soon reveals the deficits in understanding. All too often, those who work with children and adults with learning difficulties rely on check lists based on a developmental progression of learning in certain skill areas. Children who are autistic do not learn along the lines of normal development and gaps occur in all areas. It would be an impossible task to create a check list to unearth all the problems described above as not only do they appear in isolation but they are likely to be peculiar to the individual. Nevertheless, this rather strict way of applying knowledge, and the types of misunderstandings that occur, are a hindrance to effective learning and can be missed unless staff, especially skilled at identifying them, are constantly observing and assessing behaviour.

LIFE EDUCATION

There has always been a tendency for mainstream education to offer a curriculum which is divided into specialist subjects so they can be taught in greater depth. This is particularly true of education offered between the ages of 13 and 25 years when specialization tends to increase in preparation for further education and the demands of the workplace.

This is also a time when we are learning more about ourselves as individuals, as members of groups and of the wider world. At best, much of this teaching comprises the hidden curriculum in a mainstream school. At worst, we learn through experience and experimentation, failure and success. Young people who are autistic do not learn effectively in this way – they will either fail to learn at all or acquire knowledge that is not appropriately used, especially where relations with other people are involved.

Adolescents and adults with autism continue to need education in areas which are not generally taught in other schools (nor do they need to be taught to those who learn such skills without conscious effort). And teaching will continue to need to be directed at ensuring that skills are generalized making sure that none is learned in isolation and that, if there is a potential alternative application, there should be no expectancy on the part of those around that the skill will be transferred.

Coping with bodily changes

Just as with 'normal' adolescents, it is not unusual for children who are autistic to show concern about their bodily development. Given that preservation of sameness and an adverse reaction to change are well-documented as being significant in the way children who are autistic respond to their environment, it is reasonable to expect that bodily changes occurring in adolescence will cause some distress. One young man, for example, was quite upset to discover he had pubic hair and his penis was growing.

In my experience, it is rare for young people to verbalize their worries. However, one young lady did determinedly tell staff that she was 'a girl' whenever anyone referred to her as a 'young lady', long after her body had begun to develop.

Menstruation

Although the other effects of bodily changes in adolescence are sometimes forgotten, rather more attention is usually given to the onset of menstruation. Fears as to how girls will cope are common. Because more able girls require little or no supervision for bathing and toiletting needs, they are likely to discover their first period when they are alone. Preparation is, therefore, essential though a simple description of what to expect is better than complex, gynaecological explanations. One girl used the word 'bleed-bottom' which not only seemed appropriate for her, but meant that she was able to talk about the onset of menstruation in a way which made sense to her.

Girls who are autistic are just as likely to have menstrual difficulties as any other member of the female population. It is a good idea then to keep a record of the menstrual cycle – pre-menstrual syndrome seems to be fairly common, at least in my experience. Preceding a period, programmes to eliminate behavioural difficulties are unlikely to be effective if additional problems arise as a result of hormonal imbalance.

Whenever pre-menstrual syndrome is suspected it is essential that medical advice is sought, even specialist gynaecological advice. Over-the-counter products, however, such as vitamin B6, oil of Evening Primrose and the like may alleviate less severe problems. A low-dose form of the birth pill may be helpful in regulating periods or reducing those which are particularly heavy (bearing in mind the possibility of adverse effects). Preparations, such as Cyclogest and Duphaston, are available on prescription to alleviate symptoms of pre-menstrual syndrome.

Where pre-menstrual syndrome is suspected or the potential side effects of treatment is a possibility, the fact that even the most verbal young person may not be able to explain how she feels should always be borne in mind. The menstrual cycle does need to be monitored and, where someone is incapable of planning for this, there should be arrangements made in order that it can be done for them. It is not intrusive: menstruation is not usually a taboo subject amongst women, rather a subject of constant and open debate.

'Wet dreams'

Another consequence of the physical changes taking place in adolescence, for which young men may need to be prepared, is the involuntary emission of semen ('wet dreams'). One very able lad thought he had begun to urinate during his sleep. He tried to hide the evidence and was distressed in case he was thought 'a baby'. It was a simple task to explain that it was in fact not 'naughty' but 'grown up' and that any necessary washing should be dealt with in the appropriate manner.

Whilst some may disagree, we found it helpful for staff to share their own experiences in a private 'chat' with individuals. For young people who experience life in very concrete terms, 'everybody' is an abstract and meaningless concept. To have someone they know to be a responsible adult saying 'it happens to me' can be reassuring. The more socially aware the young person is, the more aware he will be that he is 'different'. There is no reason why he should be allowed to feel physical differences exist as well.

Discretion about bodily functions

We live in a society where so many of the bodily functions are taboo subjects. Because people with autism are not known for their inhibitions, considerable emphasis needs to be placed on learning not only about personal privacy but about those topics which should be treated with some discretion. To prevent her telling all present in a very loud voice, one young woman had to be taught to whisper when letting staff know her period had started. Unless explicitly taught, young people are unlikely to know it is possible to ask an adult for a private conversation in another room, away from the crowd. People with autism have enough difficulty understanding what they experience directly without being expected somehow to know that certain issues are more usually discussed behind closed doors.

Masturbation

The adolescent activity which seems to cause people most fear and embarrassment is masturbation. It should not be forgotten that very young babies are capable of erections and they are not necessarily evidence of overt sexual desire. With the onset of menstruation and the growth of reproductive organs, it is not surprising that the adolescent's attention is drawn to his or her genitalia nor, if masturbation is pleasurable, that it should be a frequent occurrence.

Young people with autism are not aware of the way in which others view them or the unspoken rules governing social conduct: it is important young people are made aware of the need for privacy and finding the right place. Masturbation should not be discouraged though as it is likely to be the only sexual pleasure most people with autism will experience. Nevertheless, even the most able person develops repetitive habits which, where there is the risk of causing soreness or of interfering with other activities, may need to be limited.

Personal hygiene

Young people with autism lack the judgement necessary to know when to change clothes, have a bath or comb their hair; neither do they pick up disapproving cues from other people. As children grow into adulthood, not only may they become less physically appealing, but their manner can cause others to regard them with a certain wariness. For more able young people, capable of taking part in a wider social life, it is important their appearance does not serve to distance them further, if they are to gain the tolerance and acceptance of other people.

Physical development at adolescence means that hygiene becomes even more important. For young people who have a level of independence which allows them privacy in matters of self-care, and where they take some pride in this, it can feel very intrusive if an adult suddenly begins to increase supervision; hence the importance of establishing appropriate routines at an early stage. Daily bathing and the use of deodorants should be routine by the time a young person reaches adolescence as should a complete change of clothing. By the time such habits are seen to be necessary, they will have become far more difficult to establish. Take the young man, living as part of a group in a flat with reduced supervision who, at the age of 19, was noted to have very greasy hair. His self-care skills had not needed close monitoring for some years so that, when reminded about his hair, he said it was 'alright' as he had 'washed it on Wednesday' – six days earlier. Because he had just begun to stay away from home at weekends, no-one had thought to alter his routine in the residential placement to include washing his hair on Friday and Sunday evenings.

Although good hygiene and diet can help to reduce skin problems, a number of adolescents suffer from acne. At worst, this can cause scarring for life and medical advice should be sought at the earliest possible stage. The young people concerned may not be bothered about their appearance but other people may be put off; any practical measures which can be taken to ease integration should be considered.

Health

Good health care should be seen as an essential part of someone's life. Where young people have and are encouraged to maintain personal privacy, there may be problems which arise unseen. Just because able young people have good use of language and have acquired a degree of independence, it does not follow they will recognize or be able to explain symptoms of ill health.

There is a need to ensure that young people living in sheltered accommodation can discriminate between, on the one hand, professional people who can advise them (or people they know well enough to confide in) and, on the other, people with whom it is not acceptable to discuss more personal issues. It is a good idea to arrange for regular physical check-ups by someone known to be a 'professional' – in this way privacy can be maintained. Nevertheless, it is also important to encourage young people to confide in staff who, in turn, need to be very careful to promote appropriate behaviour. For instance, one young man of 22 noticed he had some sore patches in the groin area and told a houseparent. Rather than insist he show her, she asked what he wanted to do about it – one option was that he arrange an appointment with a doctor. It was his decision to ask her to examine the patches instead, 'just in case there's nothing wrong'. Had a male member of staff been available, it would perhaps have been more appropriate to ask him to help out.

SOCIAL SKILLS

More able young people will have some grasp of what is 'normal' – they will copy others because it is only themselves they see as different. Young people can and do feel isolated from the social interactions of others; it is important, therefore, that they learn socially acceptable conduct, not behaviour which will isolate them still further.

Social communication

Social communication is something people who are autistic find most difficult. It is also the problem most likely to isolate them from life in the community. We can only teach rules not judgement, and those of us who mix with people regularly know the unspoken social signals we exchange can be very subtle – hard to read and easy to get wrong. So much of what we say is left unsaid. It is easy for people who are autistic to misinterpret intended messages. Unfinished sentences, gestures, facial expressions convey meanings which are lost on them.

Help can be given to enable young people to integrate more easily into social situations. Teaching young people to listen and to make appropriate social responses such as 'that's nice' or 'what a pity' is valid. A good listener does not remain immobile and silent. We are all more likely to continue talking when other people have a way of acknowledging they are listening.

But even the most able young people with autism have difficulty in holding conversations. Either they offer limited replies or are so long-winded in their attempt to give a complete answer that they come across as boring. Their own conversational gambits tend to be inappropriate: questions may be too personal or attempts to sustain a conversation falter as they fail to pick up and respond to other people's cues. As one parent remarked, 'at best, the autistic person is a poor listener'.

Children with autism may also need to be taught to make it clear when they don't understand. This can be promoted in teaching situations, early in the child's life. Because it is all too easy for people who are autistic to focus on anything but the main point, it may be necessary to tell them when they have not understood and encourage them to use an appropriate means of signifying this.

Whereas it is possible to teach the basic sequence of introductory remarks we all tend to follow when meeting someone new, negotiating these formalities successfully still relies very heavily on responding appropriately to the way people have picked up their cues or are leading the conversational exchange. I realized just how difficult this can be for people with autism when one young man accompanied me to a buffet lunch where a local firm was to present the school with a hi-fi system. Within the confines of his home-base, this pupil could hold quite complex conversations. I had thought that he would show similar prowess at the event, particularly as he loved music. He also had a good deal of knowledge about computers and the people we were to meet worked with them. Further, they were also likely to be sympathetic to the young man's difficulties. However, I soon realized his conversational technique was strongly associated with facts he already knew about the lives of people he knew. With people he had never met, he could not latch on to common points of interest.

Nonetheless the same young man had a varied social life. From about 16 years of age he proved to be an exceptional snooker player. A member of staff who was also a keen player introduced him to the local Working Men's Club. Here he was accepted for his skill at the game – any need for communication was centred around congratulatory or sympathetic remarks and discussions about the game. Subsequently he began jogging and became a member of a local runners' club. The last I heard he was about to take up golf. All his hobbies were to some extent obsessional, but he was also extremely skilled at them. In becoming a member of specialist clubs he was able to socialize with others as obsessed as himself!

Vulnerability

Once young people begin to go out alone, it is their vulnerability that is the prime cause for concern. Because the aim for people who are autistic ought to be maximum independence, early education should reflect this objective. If people with autism are able to manage road crossings, public transport and handle money, a wider life-style is open to them. However, they are also at risk from those in the community who exploit their innocence.

The school where I worked contained a flat for young people capable of living with less supervision than the rest of the school. Their vulnerability was emphasized when a man made sexual advances to one young female resident. She knew him as a 'friend' through the place where she worked as a volunteer at weekends. Luckily, because she was someone who never liked physical contact in any form, she apparently reacted in no uncertain terms. The matter only came to light some months later when she made a chance comment, 'you mustn't tell if people touch you, or you'll get into trouble'. This presented staff with a dilemma. Years of work had gone into teaching this young person to accept at least people brushing past her, or not to react to a hand on or an arm around her shoulder. How to teach what kind of touching is 'right' and what is 'wrong'?

Because of the difficulties young people with autism have in transferring and generalizing skills, 'role-play' was generally felt to be an inappropriate teaching method. However, an enterprising member of staff decided there were ways in which it could be made to work. Staff discussed with the group what constituted a 'stranger' for them, and described the sorts of behaviour they might encounter. Friends of staff were invited in to play the part of someone attempting the initial stages of contact – someone touching a knee when travelling on a train for example. The young people were given instruction in how to cope – what to say and do. Attempts were made to help them distinguish between friendly contacts and those which could lead to abuse, or which were at the very least unacceptable and to which most people would respond negatively.

Films and a talk from the local Crime Prevention Officer were helpful. The Officer, however, was not familiar with autism. When he asked if they had understood, the flat group all nodded whilst, at the same time, staff shook their heads. They knew that particular issue had not been understood. This was borne out when the Officer asked what they would do if, whilst the houseparent was out, a stranger came to the door and said he wanted to come in. The answer was, 'ask him in and make him a nice cup of coffee'!

ADOLESCENCE AS A TRANSITION TO ADULTHOOD

Is adulthood reached at a moment in time or is it recognizable by levels of skill and behaviour? Within our culture, adolescence tends to be seen as a period of physiological development during which personality and behaviour change. However, this is not a universal perception. It has been argued that the psychological impact of adolescence is more dependent on cultural than biological influences. And for young people who have severe difficulties in understanding underlying social rules, the psychological impact is likely to be that much greater.

In some societies, rituals mark the time when a child becomes an adult. Our own society somehow expects young people to come to terms with the unspoken law that, over a long but indeterminate period of time, the rules governing their lives alter. There are no set guidelines and the way in which the rules are applied is very dependent on other people's expectations. If the 'normal' adolescent has difficulty in coping with these expectations during that limbo period between childhood – a time when rules are reasonably clear-cut – and adult independence, how much more difficult is it for adolescents who have only a limited grasp of the social norms which guide contact?

Something that is very evident when talking to young people with autism is that the boundaries still need to be drawn. A high level of anxiety is commonly observed but, just as with the child who continuously lines up cars, the more they are allowed to indulge their obsessions, the more they will. Some very able young people become extremely depressed. They see the life that is not available to them. It is not available at a practical level because they do not have the practical skills, but it is also inaccessible because of the nature of autism.

The adult model

From an early age, all children learn that adults have a special place in their lives. They are the people who make the rules. For people who are autistic, the 'adult' tends to be a rather more important figure for a longer period. Young people who have difficulty in relating to others will have better relationships with those who are tolerant of their handicaps and who attempt to establish empathic contact. People with autism also need rather stricter rules to live by than is usual and, where these are unequivocally applied, adults become associated with a certain ability to control. They can offer a degree of security and continuity in a very uncertain world.

More able children, however, tend to associate adulthood with 'normality'. And, given that phrases such as 'you're too young' or 'grow up' are commonly used by adults, it is not surprising that young people who are dissatisfied with the apparently arbitrary restrictions on their liberty will long for the day when this world of freedom is open to them. The model of perfection is often the adult who makes the rules, be it parent or member of staff. To a person who is autistic, achieving adulthood must seem like paradise! A time when the rules will no longer apply.

For the young person who wants this freedom, the desire to be an adult can provide an extra motivation to learn new skills. It is particularly helpful if it can be shown that they do not have but need certain skills. At the same time, the desire to be an adult can bring problems. People with autism do not see the limitations on their own lives let alone those on other people; they may continue to want total freedom without considering either their own difficulties or other people's needs and feelings.

Applying adult rules

In a school which offered work facilities beyond 19 years of age, it was possible to observe how the attitude of more able people with autism changed as they approached school-leaving age. It was almost as if the adolescent rebellion had begun – the rules no longer applied to them. Although the rules were not flouted in a genuinely anti-social way, there was a determination to be an adult. What 'adult' meant to these young people was not always obvious.

One young man, about to leave school, began to refuse to comply with simple requests. He was not only argumentative but made his points with some force: they were less requests open to negotiations than demands. Adopting a rational approach of talking through the demands with him did not help because he could not see another person's point of view. Nor could he 'see' the restrictions on his life. We wondered what we had been teaching in our school, geared as we had supposed it was to meeting the needs of children with autism. To this end, however, staff had had of necessity to make demands rather than requests of younger children and to raise their voices in order to draw attention to the language being used. It transpired that he thought adults were never themselves told what to do. For him 'told' also meant 'asked'. In other words, we all go around doing and saying what we want, when we want.

The same young man saw the main advantage of being adult as receiving a brown envelope which he knew contained money and which he could put into a bank account. Most of all, he wanted to pay a mortgage and an electricity bill! The facts of life were easily explained when it was pointed out just how much these cost and how little would then be left to indulge his hobbies of photography, video games and pop records.

The perception that young man had of staff never being told what to do was more difficult to correct. It was explained that everyone had bosses but, again, it was outside his experience to grasp the subtleties of hierarchical relationships. Initially, staff working alongside him made a great point of demonstrating the pecking order: senior staff told others what to do in his presence. Anyone visiting the head-teacher's office made a great fuss about the possibility of being in trouble. He was shown job descriptions and given his own; a simplified disciplinary procedure was explained. Anything outside his own personal experience was a mystery to this young man, neither could he believe what he was told – a little like asking the rest of us to believe that there is life on Mars. He needed to be shown and to experience for himself that the unseen rules did exist.

The types of friendships that develop amongst people who are autistic often involve mutual obsessions. The friendship between two particular young men seemed to have resulted in a joint rebellion against staff, arising out of the issue of who dictated whether or not they should go to the toilet. The young men had evidently discussed the matter and were firm in their opinion that 'they won't let me go to the toilet'. The individual circumstances were revealed during private interviews with each young man. One had something of a phobia about toilets, being anxious in case they had not been flushed before he used them. Consequently, he frequently asked to go but often did not get beyond the doorway. This had resulted in times being imposed when he was required to go into the toilet and when staff were on hand to offer reassurance. The other young man had asked to use the toilet at a public swimming pool just as he was getting into a minibus with the group to return home. He was asked to wait. For both these young people the 'rules' had not been adequately explained.

Although people with autism need rules, it is more difficult to provide them when the issues are abstract. One young man had a tendency to touch large women. He moved too close to them and put his hands on their waists. He had been known to kiss them or touch their legs. Because women recognized he was 'different' they did not react normally, that is told him to go away. He had been given rules about not being allowed to touch new acquaintances but he still needed to know 'what is a friend?'; 'what is a stranger?'; 'how many times do you have to talk to someone before you know them?'. These questions do not have definitive answers, but they need tackling in terms the person with autism can understand. And, just as a child who has greater learning difficulties would be restrained, so we must intervene in episodes of socially unacceptable behaviours involving young people who are more able. Moreover, providing rules helps to ease the confusion experienced in situations where young people cannot make sense of socially significant cues and signals.

Promoting adult realism

The verbal child with autism begins to express future aspirations in the same way as a young 'normal' boy might say he wants to be a fireman when he grows up. The problem with young people who are autistic is that 'I want to' is likely to mean 'I will'. The desire is not modified by any insight into their own limitations, the attainability of their ambition, or by other people's control of their lives – be this explicit or implicit.

People with autism seldom perceive the rationale behind arguments; often they fail to grasp the unspoken limitations on fulfilling their ambitions. At these times, it is important they discover 'no' means 'no'. Given the more subtle ways in which this is supposed to be inferred, it is far easier for the young person who has learnt at an early age that there are restrictions on freedom, and that other people enforce them, to see that this principle continues to apply in adulthood. The late teenage years are as much a check-point into freedom for the person with autism as they are for the 'normal' person. Everyone goes to school and there the rules are explicit. Leaving school is the actual point of entry into adult life, full of opportunities for real decision-making, personal choice and seemingly limitless freedom.

There are some people whose handicaps and behaviour fall within the autistic spectrum of conditions who are able to take part in certain practical or social activities in the community. There are also many who can verbalize the wish, but may never be able to put it into practice. For instance, it is not unusual for young people to want to drive a car (this is seen as being 'adult') and neither is it unusual for those around them to postpone disappointment by saying you cannot, by law, drive a car until 17 years of age. With their literal interpretation of language coupled with a distorted view of their own potential, young people with autism are likely to believe either they will be able to drive at 17 years of age, or at least be able to start taking lessons. Perhaps it is better to say 'no' to such requests at the outset. Then, if the time ever came when it were possible, it would be a special event. Told 'no', they may continue to want to drive a car, but will not expect it to happen.

For most young people with autism, however, the concept of freedom does not necessarily incorporate a desire to live away from home. Indeed, home is where rules tend to be relaxed and this is only to be expected. Not only have young people had more time to practise their need to 'preserve sameness' there but parents have other commitments and cannot impose such a rigid regime as can staff whose relations with the young people are uncomplicated by feelings of emotional attachment or guilt. Even where young children with autism live away from home, it is easy for staff to become tolerant of autistic behaviour which may not be regarded so leniently elsewhere. From an early age, young people likely to need long-term shelter and protection should be prepared accordingly. Leading them to believe they may well have a home of their own, or be able to live with parents for the rest of their lives, is unrealistic and unhelpful.

So many young people become dissatisfied with their lot as they approach adulthood. They begin to question the restrictions on their lives and they need answers. They need the opportunity to talk, on their own terms, about the difficulties they encounter. Discussion must always be couched in concrete terms but it must not be avoided. A happy young man can soon become unhappy and resentful because, for him, adulthood was supposed to be being, doing, saying as he wanted. He needs to know why this is not possible. Often it may mean telling him 'this is so, because I say so': lengthy discussion framed in philosophical or psychoanalytical terms has no meaning. At the same time, the adolescent or young adult must be treated with the respect we accord everyone reaching maturity. He needs the opportunity to express his aspirations and to be given reasons why they are not attainable, if this is the case.

Recognizing and accepting restrictions

Young people who have a vague grasp of what is 'normal' often know that they are unable to compete in some areas. It is unfair to ignore the potential barriers to leading a fully independent life when they themselves are aware they exist, albeit unseen, to prevent them from doing as they wish. Does any of us have a right to social acceptance or having all our wishes granted? If someone says she can cook and can therefore live on her own, it is necessary to point out the skills she does not have but needs, if she is to be independent.

More able young people need reasons for not having their freedom – in the sense that we try to develop skills to equip young people for 'real' life. Part of this process is to learn to recognize one's own limitations. It may mean having to say 'because I say so' some of the time, but that is reality too. It may not be expressed in words but we know that barriers exist without having to be told. People with autism do not. It is not surprising that young adults begin to rebel against the rules set by staff – where autism prevents a realistic view of life, staff are the kill-joys.

A very useful practice is that of encouraging 'normal' young people of a similar age to socialize with more able young people with autism. Well-primed, they are able to talk about their own lives and the restrictions they experience, as well as drawing attention to the advantages being in protected living accommodation brings by way of friendships, outings, entertainment and staff to take on many domestic tasks, or at least people with whom to share them. Some young people may be disillusioned by descriptions of the big outside world, but this kind of socializing can help them come to terms with their own situation.

SEXUALITY AND PERSONAL RELATIONSHIPS

Establishing what is right or wrong in relationships between individuals is never easy. Non-handicapped people are just as likely to experience difficulties in understanding their own feelings and behaviour, and that of other people, as do people with learning difficulties. For people who are severely impaired in their ability to relate to others, to empathize and exercise appropriate judgement, there are likely to be even greater difficulties.

Social/sexual conduct

Inappropriate social behaviour rather than overt sexual advances is likely to be the cause of most difficulties. One young lad knocked on every door in his street to see if there was someone in the house who would be his girl-friend. Another, having seen men with their arms round girls, began to cuddle female members of staff and stroke their hair. Some young people may retain earlier obsessions. It is very difficult to explain to a member of the public that a young man is feeling the stocking rather than making a sexual advance. That is why such behaviour needs to be controlled at an early age.

Establishing guidelines becomes particularly important in those social situations where more able young people find themselves without the protection of a known adult to offer sympathetic advice. The problem lies in their inability to relate effectively to people, to recognize interpersonal signals – whether encouraging or discouraging – and to know what to do about them either way. This is what causes most anguish for those young people who want girl-friends or boy-friends because that is part of being adult.

Sexual rights

Whether or not everyone, including people with a severe mental handicap, has a right to sexual fulfilment is the subject of current debate. Should we promote sexual contacts? If so, who should be the partner? What is a consenting adult? Is it realistic to expect to have a girl-friend or boy-friend, or a sexual relationship, just because it is desired?

In fact, it is more likely that those people with autism who have the most independence, involved as they are in everyday social contact, will require support and sympathetic understanding for their failure to create and maintain relationships.

Sexual relationships

If a young person who is autistic expresses a desire for a partner, it should not necessarily be equated with a wish for a sexual relationship. Surprisingly perhaps, although some young people have been told about physical sexual contact, the information has not then been translated into a desire for sexual intercourse. This may be because shared physical sexual expression has not been part of their experience or that, where they wish to copy adults, explicit sexual behaviour is, in general, not seen. The young man who says he wants a girl-friend tends to be saying just that, rather like the young man who wanted to pay a mortgage. It is a literal statement devoid of the usual connotations of an intimate relationship between two people. Having a girl-friend or boy-friend is seen as part of becoming an adult, and there is no doubt that many young people see being an adult as the answer to all their problems.

Peer friendships

For all that people with autism lack judgement, have difficulty in appreciating another's viewpoint and in recognizing the limitations imposed on everyone's life – they are aware of some of the opportunities available to the non-autistic person. Some of these are practical such as being able to join in activities carried out by other people of their own age, others are emotional. The latter are likely to remain inaccessible to young people who cannot relate effectively enough to gain the friendships they most often desire.

Many feel very lonely. There is no doubt more able young people with autism want friends, but have no real conception of what friendship is. There are no set rules for making friends. Most of us are aware that some of the closest friendships we make arise out of feelings of empathy or what we might even describe as 'chemistry'. Other relationships depend on shared interests. Most come to be sealed with shared feelings. Although the emotional dimension of friendship is unlikely to be available to people with autism, they can feel rejected if they see themselves as not having friends. Young people with autism placed in schools for more socially aware children can be very unhappy. Their vulnerability in situations where they cannot judge what is right or wrong, coupled with a tendency to accept any social contact – good or bad – because they see it as 'normal' can make their lives a misery. They may slavishly follow instructions to do something others would immediately recognize as being unacceptable and then be reprimanded without understanding why. They say they do not have friends but at the same time they do not know what a friend is.

For young people with this type of social difficulty, adopting a policy of telling them who their friends are and why is helpful. The concept of friendship needs to be explained in terms of people doing things together. People with autism have a one-way route of communication. Another person who is autistic may not be bored by this, or may even enjoy the repetitiveness. Judging by the popular interests in pop music, transport and computers amongst more verbal and more able young people, shared obsessions are a possibility. It is important to promote these contacts and actually to say 'he is your friend because he talks to you about . . . '. It may be rather dictatorial but my justification is that young people who have hitherto felt themselves to be friendless can then say they have friends.

Befriending a person with autism

The way in which people who are autistic see other people making friends is very important. Those who work with children sharing these difficulties tends to develop a larger-than-life persona – they are often loud, effusive and extrovert. These are almost essential qualities for staff working with young people who have difficulty, not only in recognizing they are the person being addressed, but also in interpreting the attitude of others towards themselves. One young man was very unhappy because, as he put it, 'Maria isn't friendly to me, she doesn't speak to me'. Maria was a very young, very shy worker. She was friendly, but rather quiet. She said 'hello', but tended not to follow this up with lengthy conversation. What Maria was not doing, because of her own shyness, was making the second move in social interaction. The young man did not make the first move because of his autism. Friendliness to him was the way other people made a great play of communicating with him. If they did not do this he neither saw the need to do anything about it himself, nor indeed did he see it as his place to do so. For this young man, only effusive social contact from other people equated with liking him, quiet approaches did not.

Counselling

The difficulties described so far can lead to a high level of anxiety and/or depression which may need treatment. Counselling can help but needs to take account of the lack of insight and empathy which are part of the autistic handicap. Normal counselling techniques suggest the practitioner should neither judge nor dictate but, to be effective, these are necessary approaches to adopt in counselling a young person who is autistic. An understanding of the autistic person-ality and of the way people with autism think is essential if counsel-ling is to help. For instance, because the echolalic nature of language seems to continue, it is possible to select out their own positive view-point and then feed it back with a fair chance of it becoming positive thought.

The same goes for feelings. One young man always worried. He worried about being worried, and then worried about that. Talking to him about this and trying to discover a reason for it was futile. Worrying was his obsession. He needed to talk about it but, by setting a time limit, it was possible to contain his unhappiness. When it showed, telling him he looked happy was very effective. He could be thoroughly enjoying himself but mention of the word 'worry' meant he immediately became worried. Positive reinforcement of his happy times helped him to recognize his own enjoyment. A positive attitude adopted by those around him was reflected back.

There are others for whom this technique will not have any effect and psychiatric treatment may be necessary. Even then, this should be supported by someone who understands that, in common with other people who are autistic, those who are more able can have unusual reactions to tranquillizers and other drugs.

PSYCHIATRIC ILLNESSES

The possibility of psychiatric illnesses should not be discounted amongst the more able group. There are some people who cope with a 'normal' life-style and, if we measure success in terms of educational attainment, achieve success. Some may gain places at university to study subjects in which they are exceptionally skilled. Yet, as Lorna Wing states in a paper on Asperger's syndrome (see p.104), 'clinically diagnosable anxiety and varying degrees of depression may be found, which seem to be related to a painful awareness of handicap and difference from other people'. More able young people are often well aware that somehow they are different and, because they have an obsessive nature which creates repetitive thought patterns, it is not surprising that the person who is trying to cope independently – without the protection of another person who understands and can help compensate for the difficulties – finds life not only confusing but a very unhappy state to be in. Lorna Wing's study of 18 young people diagnosed as having Asperger's syndrome (quoted above) included 13 who had already been referred to adult services because of superimposed psychiatric conditions. And such conditions are likely to arise when one considers the awareness required of a 'normal' adult in order to appreciate the way in which other people might think, act, react and to be able to predict cause and effect.

I once spoke to a lady whose son had committed suicide because he was so unhappy with his life. He had not been diagnosed as suffering any particular handicap, mental or psychological, but listening to her description of him, it seemed he had very severe difficulties in relating to others, communicating effectively, and had been very obsessive at both sophisticated and simple levels. He also had an IQ of 130+ and this may have served to disguise some of his underlying problems. He had frequently asked his mother for rules in areas which the rest of us would accept as grey. As a very attractive and intelligent young man, he had not been without admirers and one young woman had very obviously been interested in him as a potential boy-friend. He had not picked up the cues and, when she wrote him a note to explain why she had given up the pursuit, he was the one who felt rejected. It was not this single event which caused him to take his life but a culmination of experiences arising out of his inability to see life from anyone else's view-point except his own.

CRIMINAL ACTS

Some people in the more able group may be 'at risk' for other reasons. In spite of their abilities, the obsessional drive of people with autism can overwhelm them. One young man who was virtually able to manage independently and had always taken great pride in his achievements, particularly in number skills, ran out of a shop without waiting for change. The member of staff who happened to be nearby at the time realized that he was dashing out to watch the traffic lights change! How would this have been regarded had he not already paid for his shopping?

The problems that can arise where such bizarre behaviour exists alongside well-developed social skills are obvious. But what of those young people whose obsessions are rather more anti-social? Given that people who are autistic have such great difficulties in exercising choice or judgement, it must be said that, on the whole, asocial rather than anti-social is the appropriate term. Although in other people, obsessional or repetitive behaviour can result in neurosis, people who are autistic are, in general, unaware that their behaviour is a problem and so lack the desire to change it.

'Anti-social' obsessions may be more readily accepted in the less able person who is, at the same time, more obviously handicapped. Because greater supervision is built in, the problems are also more easily managed in settings for people who are less independent. Eccentricity is accepted in many people but what happens if an obsession with cars develops into driving them away no matter who the owner is; 'collecting' leads to stealing; a fascination with fire results in arson?

An example of the potential to carry out criminal acts is the case of a young woman who had, for some time, been interested in fire engines. She had already called out the fire brigade on a false alarm. Recognized to be 'different', she was given a bar of chocolate and told not to call the fire brigade unless there was a real fire. So she did just that, having lit it herself! (This was only realized later and police took a lenient view.) She later set fire to the fence between her own home and a neighbour. The neighbour decided to remonstrate and told her that if the petrol on the drive had caught light she would be dead and as black as the fence. Although upset by this, it did not prevent her from setting light to a lower bunk-bed, while her sister was sleeping above, and running from the house to watch the fire engines arrive. She showed no emotion about the consequences and, indeed, having been told what could have happened, she greeted her mother with the remark 'Oh, I thought you'd be all black and burned'. For her own and others' safety this young woman is now in a secure environment which at least meets her needs better than the prison where she had to spend six months awaiting transfer to a more appropriate centre.

It should not be assumed that all young people capable of living more independently are likely to engage in criminal activities. The above example is only given to illustrate how the obsessive impulses young people with autism have are not inhibited by the more basic and obvious social rules. How much more difficult then is it for them to grasp the subtle conventions which govern our everyday lives?

CONCLUSION

The future well-being of people who are autistic depends very much on their own capacity to adapt to the needs of others, or at least accept that others will have some jurisdiction over their lives. They need to develop a philosophical attitude of some kind, to learn to feel 'it doesn't matter'. This is hard because there is a great divide between what does and does not matter. For young people who have limited judgement as to how far their desires can be accommodated or how realistic these are, it does matter.

Skills are important if they offer openings into a social life which would otherwise be unattainable. They can occasionally give access to a highly selective job-market, though it remains important to ensure that those working alongside have some understanding and tolerance of the problems experienced by people with autism.

Because determining 'right' and 'wrong' behaviour is a relative rather than an absolute judgement, requiring the particular circumstances to be weighed up before reaching any conclusion, it is a difficult concept to teach. There are times when explanations are ineffective because they rely on judgement and insight into other people's needs and feelings. So many decisions about how we act, about how we respond, or about when not to respond are reached as if by instinct. This is what young people who are autistic find most difficult. They do not have this instinct. They cannot weigh up the subtleties.

Nevertheless, they are people with needs and feelings of their own. Whatever protection is given, it is most important that these young people take part in as much of life as is available to them whilst, at the same time, having the security of someone nearby who can provide and explain the rules, and who, above all, is accepting of the autistic personality others may reject.

FURTHER READING

AHTACA (1985) *The Special Curricular Needs of Autistic Children*, AHTACA, London.

Dewey, M. and Everard, M. (1974) The near-normal autistic adolescent. *Journal of Autism and Childhood Schizophrenia*, **4** (4), Dec., 348–56.

National Autistic Society (1988) *Selection of Papers Presented at a Seminar on Asperger Syndrome*, NAS, London.

Newson, E. (1980) The Socially Aware Autistic Child, paper presented at Warwick Conference, NAS, London.

Schopler, E. and Mesibov, G.B. (1983) *Autism in Adolescents and Adults*, Plenum Press, New York.

Tantam, D. (1987) *A Mind of One's Own*, NAS, London.

Wing, L. (1981) Asperger syndrome: a clinical account. *Journal of Psychological Medicine*, **11** 115–29.

5

Adolescence and early adulthood (2): The needs of the young adult with severe difficulties

Alison Elliot

As indicated in Chapter 1, autism is now recognized as a descriptive term for a spectrum of related disorders, otherwise known as the 'autistic continuum'. This chapter will focus on the specific characteristics and needs of the adolescents and adults who are not only socially impaired but have other severe learning difficulties.

Although there are obviously individual differences according to physical development, personality, experience, and ability, people with autism who have severe learning difficulties tend to engage little in social interaction, have little communicative ability (being either non-verbal or considerably echolalic in speech), have stereotyped hand and spinning behaviours and, frequently, unusual responses to sensory experience such as indifference to pain or fascination with lights. Most of these young people do not have particular skills or hobbies.

Whereas young people with autism continue to have special needs, these may change significantly at adolescence as physical changes occur and the influence and demands of society changes. Considerable support and the systematic teaching of life skills will be required. Without outside help, the adolescent with autism does not simply 'grow up'.

Physical changes in adolescence can be very disturbing, and this is particularly so for young people who may not be able to question, or even perceive, changes in people around them. The rate of development varies from family to family and individual to individual making preparation for change difficult. And, in any case, the inability of many people with autism to conceptualize past and present severely limits the value of any sort of preparation. Carers may need to demonstrate in very practical and concrete ways how to cope with bodily changes: siblings and others known to the person with autism can provide useful role models in areas of personal hygiene.

Emotional development and social behaviour are more difficult because they are less tangible. It is often easier to give people strategies for coping with situations, such as relaxation or breathing exercises, rather than helping people to understand why they feel unhappy, anxious, or excited.

HEALTH

Epilepsy

Of particular significance to young people with autism as they approach adolescence is the possibility of the onset of epilepsy. And there is a higher occurrence rate in the less able group. Research suggests that between a quarter and a third of people who have an IQ of less than 70 and are autistic will develop seizures.

In many cases, seizures are completely controllable with medication. Also, a pattern of fits tends to develop which in turn helps in their management. For example, fits may occur during illness, in the early morning, following sudden weight increase, at the time of menstruation or during periods of excitement or anxiety. A few young people are able to signal an approaching fit but, more likely, anticipation will depend on the carer recognizing the signs.

Frequently, however, there may be no warning. To the extent that many young people are under constant, if unobtrusive, supervision, it is possible to minimize the risks. It is, of course, important that the carer is familiar with the individual's response to seizures and knows what to do. Some people will need particularly close support both during and after a seizure. For instance, it may be advisable to have on hand valium suppositories or other individual requirements. These can be kept in a simple container and slipped into a coat pocket for example.

Monitoring of seizures and regular consultation with the supervising physician are vital. Carers need to be alert to the possible side effects of drugs as well as to any changes in behaviour which can be observed over a period of time.

Diet

Research has shown that young people become less active between the ages of 11 and 14, an observation endorsed by many parents of adolescents with autism. This is probably why some young people are over-weight. One study of children showed that the child with autism took in a significantly greater amount of nutrients (with the exception of vitamins A and C) than the control group. Other factors in weight gain may include the side effects of drugs or ritualistic eating habits. All adolescents need large amounts of calories and, although young people with autism also increase their appetite, they frequently do not then reduce their food intake later in adulthood. It would seem that this period of adolescence can be the beginning of a sometimes ongoing struggle to prevent over-weight.

Parents have also speculated that a relationship between diet and behaviour exists. Allergic reactions to certain foods have been suggested as an explanation for sudden outbursts of aggressive or unacceptable behaviour. Other behaviours associated with autism, such as excessive drinking of fluids and irregular eating patterns, may cause ill health. In order to reduce unnecessary problems such as tooth decay, or common ailments such as colds, constipation and so on, which can cause both discomfort and a deterioration in behaviour, it is very important to ensure every individual has as healthy a diet as possible. This can be difficult as food fads are not only frequent amongst people with autism but, in my experience, are not 'grown out of' as one would expect. Nor, given the difficulty people with autism have in understanding the consequences of their actions, is the concept of healthy eating easy to get across. It seems sensible therefore to encourage diets which allow for the fads but which include ways of disguising less enjoyable but necessary foods.

Signs of ill health

Sudden changes in behaviour may indicate that all is not well but health and ill health may be difficult to differentiate in people with limited self-awareness. Symptoms can be missed as they are often not presented or, if they are, may not necessarily be those normally associated with a particular illness. The young person himself or herself may not know what it is to feel ill. Asking questions will frequently produce an inaccurate or echolalic response or put the young person under pressure to provide an illness.

Most detective work has to be around external signs and past history. The person concerned may well struggle to maintain a regular routine, particularly as this may be the only form of comfort he or she can find. This can further cloud the picture as, for instance, someone with a stomach upset may go on eating food. Lack of response to pain can lead to other diagnostic problems. Patients have developed appendicitis or broken bones without visible signs of distress.

Any kind of psychiatric syndrome can occur together with autism, the commonest reportedly being depression, and a high level of anxiety is seen in some people with autism, the physical signs of which may be sweating, irregular breathing and a rapid pulse. Certain psychiatric syndromes, however, pose problems of differential diagnosis because some clinical features resemble those found in autism. For example, severe depression can cause people without developmental disorders to become withdrawn and to avoid social contact.

PERSONAL HYGIENE AND SEXUAL DEVELOPMENT

The onset of menstruation and any accompanying discomfort or hormonal changes, as well as changes in body shape and size, are difficult for young people to accommodate. Helping young people to cope with the shock of bodily changes at the same time as making the necessary adjustments to self-care routines are tasks which have to be tackled explicitly and systematically. Counselling or discussing the feelings associated with adolescence is difficult or impossible with people who have severe difficulties. Even recognizing menstrual pain, for example, usually relies heavily on the carer being able to detect changes in behavioural patterns.

Some practical preparation for managing personal hygiene should, therefore, be undertaken so that the onset of periods, for instance, does not come as a complete shock. This should be carried out in a matter of fact way by a family member or another known person so that the young person with autism comes to accept the innovation as routine. For example, some mothers deliberately take their daughters into the bathroom and demonstrate the procedure of changing sanitary protection before it is actually required.

Many young people with autism are socially innocent and, given the nature of the basic impairments, are likely to remain so. They need then to be shown socially appropriate behaviour and consistently discouraged from inappropriate discussion or behaviour. As in other areas of teaching, the underlying principle to observe is that students will be unable to understand a concept which cannot be directly experienced or to acquire a skill without outside intervention.

The teaching of personal hygiene, therefore, is best undertaken step by step, in its proper setting, at the appropriate time. Both sexes should be taught new skills within the context of their regular routines so that, as far as possible, these activities become an accepted part of their everyday life. Care must be taken not to create patterns of behaviour which, for social reasons, will have to be unlearned later.

Care needs to be exercised in interpreting inappropriate behaviour as signs of sexual awareness: one young man, for example, is very interested in women's tights to the extent that he will look up their skirts to find out if they are wearing tights or stockings. Another young man has a fixation about under-arm hair and, in the spring, when people begin to wear fewer clothes, will frequently slip his hand inside women's blouses to find out if they have hair. In my experience, the majority of young people with autism show no interest in sexual contact with others. Masturbation, therefore, seems to be the logical sexual practice for the severely disabled person with autism. Guidance and guidelines about where and when this is appropriate should be provided.

BEHAVIOUR

It should always be remembered that the problems of adults who are autistic have their roots in the basic impairments of the syndrome. However, managing behaviour problems in adults is different from managing children's behaviour. The size of the person may be intimidating even where the problems are not as extreme or as varied as those of children. Potentially aggressive behaviour can provoke a range of responses in care-givers. Tentativeness on the part of the care-giver may cause insecurity in the person with autism and lead to uncertainty and further disruptive behaviour.

Patterns of problem behaviour, which may be the product of many diverse experiences or of previous attempts at modification may, even if established only in adolescence, be extremely difficult to change. And social attitudes towards disruptive behaviour in adults are much less tolerant than towards children. Fortunately, as adolescents mature, they often grow calmer and more settled.

Social conduct

As adults, we exercise choice as to how much we conform and how many eccentricities we are prepared to reveal. Generally, however, our behaviour is governed both by the company and the situation we are in. It is this very inability to recognize the social significance of situations that gives all people with autism such profound difficulties.

Those who are able or more verbal can be offered explanations as to what they should and should not do and basic ground rules can be set. It is sometimes only necessary to remind them about the social rules governing the situation they are going to be in. For example, 'this is a church service but the choir is singing so you must listen', or, 'at the buffet, you must only take one plate of food at a time'.

For people who are less aware and for whom general guidelines may not be enough, it is often easier to be clear about where it is always appropriate to adjust your tights or tidy your shirt-tails and so on. This approach may be more limiting but is less likely to cause confusion or put people in situations where they could be subjected to verbal abuse or even physical restraint and intervention by the police. It is usually necessary to rehearse social situations again and again so that individuals not only experience waiting in a queue, for example, but, given frequent reinforcement, can do so under many different circumstances.

Lack of motivation

Some young adults who are autistic become under-active and listless. They want to stay in the house or in their own room, perhaps lying down or standing in corners doing little, if anything at all. They appear to be continually tired. If possible, it is best to try and encourage short bursts of appropriate and purposeful activity which is both stimulating and meaningful to the individual.

Stereotyped behaviour

Stereotyped behaviour is an area where considerable thought and sensitivity on the part of carers must be exercised. It may be as appropriate to allow some behaviours to continue as to prevent others. It is occasionally possible to see new types of undesired behaviour developing and to forestall them. However, in adults, it is more likely that these behaviours are either already well-established or are reappearing as the result of some external or internal stimulation.

When considering the management of these behaviours, the following questions should be asked before embarking on an intervention programme:

Do they matter?

1. Because they intrude on other people or their possessions;
2. Because they prevent the individual from doing anything else;
3. Because they are offensive to others;
4. Because the behaviour will, in the long term, cause damage or deformity to the individual concerned.

How often do they occur?

1. Are they continuous;
2. Do they occur most of the time but are easily interrupted to perform other activities or engage in more socially acceptable alternatives;
3. Do they only occur in leisure time or in other specific situations;
4. Are they a result of some temporary change, that is a period of stress.

With adults, if a behaviour really needs intervention, there is often information from the past to indicate how it may have developed and what measures have already been considered. Usually, the most successful approach is either to try and keep the behaviour within acceptable limits or to supplant it with some other activity. Given that any attempt to prevent one stereotyped behaviour will frequently provoke another, it may be of benefit to the client to ensure this actually is, if not useful, then at least less undesirable.

Stereotyped verbal behaviour can occur even where the individual has minimal speech. This may need to be carefully monitored and limited. Endless questions or catch phrases may be socially unacceptable and inhibit genuine communication.

Aggressive and disruptive behaviour

Aggressive and disruptive behaviour can be more frequent within those young people with autism who have more severe disabilities.

Outbursts may occur because the individual has very few other means of expressing his or her needs. In these cases, an alternative form of communication is required. Or, they may arise out of anxiety or fear. Fears can be as a result of change (however minimal) to the environment or they may have an apparently irrational cause. One person may have a fear of certain places, such as unfamiliar lavatories, or of large spaces, or of specific objects, such as a record player. Yet again, some fears can be directly related to unpleasant experiences, for example, balloons that burst or dogs that barked suddenly. It is possible that outbursts are the most effective manner of making feelings known. Frequently, this type of behaviour can be reinforced simply because it achieves its object – immediate attention.

In most cases, unpredictable outbursts in adults are best looked at in the context of individual daily living patterns. It may well be integral events in the daily routine which provide the flash-points, activities such as getting up in the morning, having to get out of the bath, travelling in the taxi, and so on. These are difficult to change, particularly as it may not be easy to ascertain which step in the activity is provoking the outburst. When devising management strategies, it is useful to take the person's skills into account as well as any stress points in the daily routine known to cause distress. Further, the amount of stimulation the person can tolerate needs to be considered as well as the amount of leisure time available. Last but not least, the person's likes and dislikes should be accommodated when drawing up programmes. Breaking the day down in this way helps ensure each person is, as far as possible, really having the type of daily activities that are suitable both in nature, length of time, and environment. It provides a starting point from which each person can be helped to identify and anticipate his or her daily routine. In this way, unnecessary anxieties may be allayed.

Management strategies

A behavioural approach has proven the most effective way of dealing with disruptive and aggressive behaviour. Careful observation of what is happening before and after the problem behaviour forms the basis of a management programme.

Careful management can reduce some behaviours by giving as little attention as possible to the outburst and, at the same time, by increasing the attention given to more appropriate activities.

Typically, however, behaviours are reduced but not entirely eliminated. It should also be recognized that, although behaviours seem to have stopped, they may re-occur later in life, at times of stress for example.

As people grow older, there are many unavoidable changes which fundamentally affect the life of the person who is autistic. These can be very stressful. One young man found the idea of his brother's impending wedding very traumatic. He cried frequently and appeared inconsolable. The situation was relieved when his parents took him to visit the house where the couple would live, showing him round every part of the house. Frequently, it is not enough just to warn about impending change but, as far as possible, to demonstrate in a concrete and practical manner exactly what will be happening.

Adulthood presents other significant life events, such as divorce, retirement and bereavement, which people who are autistic will not have encountered before. These will be difficult to describe in concrete terms and impossible to demonstrate or illustrate with photographs. Support and tolerance may be all that can be offered at these times.

Self-injury

One of the most distressing forms of negative behaviour is that of self-injury which can range from hand-biting to extensive and persistent head-banging. Whilst it is distressing for carers to witness, a display of emotion may compound the problem of management.

Self-injurious behaviour, like others, can serve many functions – to avoid demands, gain attention or it can be used as self-stimulation. General management of self-injurious behaviour should be based on a very consistent response and, as far as possible, a basic routine should be maintained. Restrictions placed on people exhibiting this type of behaviour may actually increase it. If self-injurious behaviour has become established, it may be expected to take a long time to ameliorate.

Some behaviours may be triggered by internal, possibly hormonal disturbances. These are not so responsive to an environmental approach. Medication may be helpful in these cases but care should be exercised both in administering and monitoring drugs as, in the case of people with autism, the results are unpredictable. In some cases, modification of the environment, along with a new or

113

modified behavioural programme, may be required as well as medication.

SOCIAL DEVELOPMENT

Some progress in acquiring social and interpersonal skills in adolescence and adulthood can be expected. Any change, however, will tend to be marked by displays of greater interest and friendliness rather than the development of the kind of interpersonal skills needed to build up a more demanding relationship than acquaintanceship. Amongst severely disabled people with autism, there may be an improvement in overall approachability but, at the same time, it must be recognized that more social demands begin to be made on people during adolescence. It is at this age that the gulf between young people with autism and other adolescents widens, for society expects more in terms of a social contribution from its teenagers and young adults. The activities available to people of this age range become more challenging, not only in their intellectual and social demands, but also in terms of the need to comply with rules. In turn, people with autism may become more tolerant and less rejecting. They are at the stage of development when they may gain more pleasure and benefit from simple social events than ever before.

Young people with autism will be changing physically from children to adults and, as discussed earlier, will need support in coping with the transition. They will need considerable help in finding appropriate social activities – musical events, visits to the cinema, family gatherings and activities involving motion are often popular. Young people will also need help in overcoming initial fears about engaging in new activities; and continuing support should be built in to control inappropriate behaviours. Simple guidelines will need to be laid down, put into practice and constantly reinforced as the group or chosen activity changes and develops. Care should be taken with some activities because, although the initial sessions may be within the grasp of the individual, they may become increasingly complex as time goes on.

Some people will still not want to be involved in any activity and cannot be encouraged to participate in more than simple, routine social events such as meals or walks. Sometimes people with autism will come into a room and observe from a distance but will disappear or become disruptive if direct approaches are made to them. One young woman would rarely come into the family room, indeed she would only come downstairs when the family was playing bridge and was sufficiently absorbed to ignore her. She would disappear immediately anyone addressed her. More frequently, however, if the environment is familiar and secure, and the approach initiated by others, people who are autistic will show an interest. However, care should be taken not to extend the contact beyond the level of tolerance.

Preparation for adult life

At the same time as services for children with autism have been developing, there has been a growing understanding that children, whatever their level of ability, require education to develop and learn skills. The requirements of adults with 'special needs' is very much less clear, and there is even less knowledge about adults with autism than about children with autism.

The majority of people with autism and severe learning difficulties will have attended special schools or units and, as other people with special needs, may leave their educational placement at 16, 19 or 25 years of age. School leaving is an important time in most people's lives, signifying transition into adulthood. For young people with autism, it is an enormous change, particularly if they have been in the same educational environment all their school life. Depending on the level of development, this can prove either a traumatic or extremely beneficial experience. One boy relaxed and improved on leaving school, particularly enjoying the increased emphasis on physical activities in his adult environment. For others, the change from the security of one teacher and helper to coping with a wider range of staff can be extremely stressful and a variety of problem behaviours may be provoked. Realistically, because there is little choice about provision at present, planned adjustment to whatever placement is available tends to be the issue.

In preparing for adult life, a clear assessment of the person is required. This should centre on individual likes, abilities, and skills as well as those areas where assistance is required. Frequently, the young person needs to make considerable adjustments to the new environment if it is going to be successful. As many people who are autistic are unable to be flexible, and have few skills with which to mediate their environment, some specific preparation is required. This may take the form of a phased introduction into the new setting although, sometimes, a gradual induction can be more disruptive to the individual. In such cases, it may be necessary to allow staff from the new setting to become familiar with features of the present environment so that the necessary routines can be set up before the client moves.

Adult needs

For the purpose of this discussion, the needs of people with autism in adult life have been divided into three sections, viz. the individual's own needs, the needs of the individual within the immediate environment and the needs of the individual within the larger community.

So far as the individual's own needs (including social and emotional needs) are concerned, they divide broadly into practical needs (self-help, health and physical needs) and the development of interests and/or hobbies. The needs of the individual within his or her immediate caring and supportive environment – the family, the group home, the day-time setting – include developing a tolerance and acceptance of others within the group or family; a recognition of others' needs; and the ability to communicate with others even though this may be limited to a simple, contextual interaction. There is too the need to acquire the ability to contribute at one's own level to the group, with assistance as required, by helping, say, in domestic activities. There is the need to occupy free time with activities which are acceptable to the rest of the group; to move around within the establishment to satisfy individual needs; to participate in family or group occasions (such as meals or celebrations) even if only briefly and with support; and to be able to undertake essential trips, such as going to the doctor, or pursuing leisure activities, using public transport.

When helping to meet the needs of people with autism in the larger community, the essential difference is that the general public is often unable to relate to people with any sort of difficulty, let alone people with bizarre or unpredictable behaviours. Because the larger community is not on the whole a supportive environment, the individual needs a higher level of independence skills in order to make use of the facilities it has to offer. People with autism also need to be made aware of which facilities they can take advantage of and of the role they are expected to play in the community. Many of the practical aspects of going about in the wider community can be taught or else appropriate support can be given at the time.

Teaching life skills

Irrespective of progress made or skills acquired, young people who are autistic remain socially handicapped. The teaching of any skill to people with autism must be responsive to the problems which arise out of the basic impairments of the syndrome. Where there are clear social rules governing action, the teaching of life skills is easier than where the rules are implicit or ambiguous.

In some circumstances, it will be possible to teach a skill by breaking it down into basic steps but, in others, the young person will need to be helped to acquire strategies for coping with or getting round a problem. Focusing attention on a specific activity and maintaining concentration is difficult for people with severe difficulties so that considerable care must be taken to ensure the task is simple and the duration of the activity gradually built up. When devising individual programmes, any secondary disabilities should be taken into account as well as the effect of personal experience. However, certain difficulties are commonly experienced by people who are autistic.

Resistance to change

The resistance to change, shown by many people with autism can affect the teaching of any skill or task. Staff need to be aware they may have to phase in new equipment or a new environment before the teaching of a new skill can be tackled. Indeed, the student may need to learn to tolerate the mere presence of a piece of equipment before attempting to use it. Just putting on protective clothing or entering a telephone box may need to be a planned step in the learning process. (One young man resisted even going near a bicycle at first but, after months of desensitizing and then learning to ride, he is now an avid bike rider.)

Unusual sensory stimulation

Unusual sensory stimulation, such as strong smells, vibration, textures, can provide strong motivation in the teaching of life skills. One aspect of the young man's pleasure in riding a bike was the stimulation he received from travelling as fast as he could. But, equally, unusual sensory stimulation can make learning skills extremely difficult. For example, walking past factories that make specific noises, darting off to touch specific textures or going from light into dark can cause unexpected problems.

117

Unusual fears or phobias

Unusual fears or phobias may require special attention. A young man's phobia about coughing caused considerable problems which only increased as people became more aware of the effect it created. They tended to look at him and apologize as they coughed which drew more attention to the behaviour. People had to be reminded not to apologize or look at him but to behave as naturally as possible. Then the difficult behaviour lessened considerably.

Communication

This is a significant area of difficulty for people who are autistic so that the use of speech to teach a new skill may be of little help. Research shows that people with autism prefer kinaesthetically or visually presented information. Therefore, pictorial or signed communication is very often appropriate. And the language used is best kept simple and direct.

Variable skill development

The characteristically patchy development of skills means a person who is autistic may be able to attain a level of competence in some activities not matched in other areas. This can lead to unrealistic expectations about overall achievement, a situation made worse in some cases by the use of appropriate echolalia, which gives the impression of greater understanding. Consequently, young people may inadvertently be placed in situations where they are unable to cope. For example, one young man with limited self-control was able to answer echolalically several questions about why he behaved in a certain way; and he frequently made statements such as, 'I promise I won't do that again'. Only somewhat later, when it was discovered he did not know the names of articles to which he had appeared to be referring – articles for which he had a completely different set of names – did staff realize he was totally unaware of the implications of what he was saying. Like other people with autism, this young man quickly mimics phrases and uses them appropriately but without understanding.

Lack of generalization of skills and learning

This is very common and has many implications. People with autism can learn precise facts but have difficulty in classifying and using information outside the context in which it was originally taught. Skills, therefore, need to be taught in 'real life' settings, the time and place for teaching being crucial to success. And, if necessary, these skills should be taught within a multitude of appropriate settings.

The failure to generalize skills is particularly noticeable in children between home and school where two completely different types of behaviour may exist. Equally, when the individual transfers from school to adult placement or residential home, his or her skills may not transfer so that a whole range of abilities may go undetected in the new environment. For instance, one young lady transferred from school to day centre and displayed no skills – including toilet training, simple table activities, cooking, swimming, even a tolerance of her own spectacles. Fortunately, these were easy to re-establish once her new staff were aware of her potential abilities.

Poor sequencing

Poor sequencing is a common difficulty for people who are autistic. The skill can be developed in the everyday environment, using daily routines and fixed patterns. Sometimes routines become disrupted and it may be some time before the consequences come to light. Sequences of events which can be represented by pictures and related to the experiences of the individual can help maintain routines, particularly those involving time. In my experience, where daily routines are not established the young people will often set up their own rituals, such as sitting on a particular seat before going out, or going from one part of the room to another by a specific roundabout route. Whilst these patterns of behaviour may not be problematic when taken individually, as part of a small group they can prove extremely disruptive.

Learning by experience

Whereas many people learn by their mistakes, this is not necessarily the case for people who are autistic. There appears to be a lack of understanding of cause and effect: people with autism are often unaware of the results of their action, including potentially dangerous situations. They may also feel responsible for events in which they had no part, either because the event occurred simultaneously with an action of his or her own or because he or she had been responsible for something similar beforehand. This may lead to people 'admitting' to some misdemeanour in which they had no part.

Motivation

Motivation for an activity is difficult to predict. Because people with autism are not always able to anticipate the results of their work, it is necessary to find either an intrinsic motivation or a pay-off which is rewarding for the person performing the task. For some people, simply getting something finished may be sufficiently motivating.

SERVICES

There is a comparatively wide range of types of facilities into which people with severe difficulties may be placed, including services for people with a mental handicap as well as some services designed specifically for people with autism. Although the availability of resources varies from area to area, there is a great shortage of places available within specialist provision.

In the past, many young people with autism were admitted to long-stay hospitals, often as children, so that their adult needs have become the responsibility of these institutions. Over the past ten years, parents have increasingly been keeping their children within the family at home and using the educational facilities available within the community; many young people with autism will have attended local special schools or units. Unfortunately the services available for adults, whether they leave at 16, 19 or 25, are minimal and as a result of hospital closures, community services for people with a mental handicap are under increasing pressure.

Within any locality, the facilities most likely to be available are adult training centres or social education centres. Traditionally, these provided sheltered environments, including work for up to several hundred people with a variety of learning difficulties. More recently 'special needs units' are being developed as part of this service to cater for the needs of adults who are less independent and need a greater level of support. These units vary in size from 12 to 20 clients, and usually cater for people with an additional physical disability, behavioural disturbance or very severe learning difficulties.

Some people with autism who are more able and flexible may

settle into the main adult training or social education centre. Success will depend greatly on the attitudes of the manager and staff of that particular centre. Some people will also be well placed within a special needs unit, although once again the manner in which it is run and the balance of need of the whole client group will influence whether or not this is an effective placement.

The need for residential placement will occur sooner or later, and very often this can only be met within a residential community or specialist placement. The needs of people with autism who are more able, more passive or more skilful can sometimes be met within the range of communities run by voluntary agencies which cater for people with other handicaps. These communities tend to be larger than specialist autistic communities and work particularly well for some people with autism where the community runs its own activities and is more clearly self-sufficient. Although the number of specialist residential facilities and communities are increasing, as the number of school leavers in the community increases, the places that become available are greatly over-subscribed.

In some areas LEAP (Life Education for the Autistic Person) projects have been set up. These can be either residential or day facilities whose aim is to offer short-term placement, usually for three years, to teach life skills to young people with autism. A problem often occurs where there are not enough appropriate facilities to move on to.

What is needed in term of life placements for young people who are autistic will vary from person to person, but there are certain principles of good practice, common to all residential facilities within the community:

1. Normalization
2. Individualization
3. Environment

I shall look only briefly at each as they are dealt with at greater length in the next chapter.

Normalization

The aim of normalization is to provide the same range of opportunities for the person with special needs as for any other person in the community. The rights of each member of the group should be observed and the life-style should be age appropriate and one that both the individual concerned and others can look upon positively. A great deal of support will be required to help people with autism use even a little of what may be available to the ordinary citizen.

Individualization

The operation of the establishment should be individual-centred. The activities of daily life should be usable at the level of ability of the client and, where needed, assistance should be available either from another person, or by the use of strategies to allow that individual to obtain his or her goal on his or her own. The life-style should enhance both the physical and personal development of the individual.

Environment

The life-style offered by the establishment will vary depending on its situation. The activities and environment should be safe to the user in terms of external hazards. By the manner in which the establishment is run, it should also be safe to others so that each individual's behavioural needs are taken into consideration.

Finally, whatever the service provided to each individual, an essential ingredient should be for the whole group to have access to a specific worker to represent the individual person with autism. This person would have a major role to play in acting as the link between services provided by different agencies and would have a continuing awareness of the past and present needs of the client so that the level of support required can be continuously assessed and adjusted.

FURTHER READING

AHTACA (1986) *The Special Curricular Needs of Autistic Children*, AHTACA, London.

Cohen, D.J. and Donnellan, A.M. (eds) (1987) *Handbook of Autism and Pervasive Developmental Disorders*, John Wiley, New York.

Journal of Autism and Developmental Disorders, issued quarterly by Plenum Press, New York and London.

Schopler, E. and Mesibov, G.B. (1983) *Autism in Adolescents and Adults*, Plenum Press, New York.

Schopler, E. and Mesibov, G.B. (1984) *The Effects of Autism on the Family*, Plenum Press, New York.

Zarkowska, E. and Clements, J. (1988) *Problem Behaviour in People with Severe Learning Difficulties*, Croom Helm, London.

6

Autism in adulthood

William Meldrum

Unlike many childhood and adolescent problems, people do not grow out of autism. Although some of the more spectacular features tend to diminish in frequency, the triad of difficulties (communication deficit, socializing problems and rigidity of thought processes) remain. There may also be limitations in other areas of major life activities such as self-care, learning, co-ordination of movement, self-direction, capacity for independent living and economic self-sufficiency. As a consequence, there is a necessity for a response to the needs of the person with autism which is of extended or lifelong duration and which, to accommodate highly idiosyncratic needs, is individually planned and co-ordinated.

Providing an effective care and education 'package' for any group of people is a challenging task. Meeting the needs of people with autism is even more testing, particularly if the response is to be developmental and progressive, not simply static and custodial. There is still much to be learnt about autism generally, whilst responding to the needs of adults with autism is a developing art, given that the post-school sector is a major growth area in care and education provision for people with autism. Although the cause and nature of autism are imperfectly understood, it is hoped that this chapter might encourage the reader to undertake the care and training, encouragement and challenge of adults with autism in a way which is not limited by incomplete knowledge or expectations.

The kinds of concepts which should be embraced are not only those which address the effects of autism but those which promote independence, self-care, social participation, self-respect and general personal enhancement. There is a significant shortage of literature which provides any practical information on how best to respond to the needs of adults with autism. Whilst recognizing that a series of books would be required to do the subject justice, perhaps this chapter will at least help the reader consider the aims of services for people with autism, the context in which these might be achieved and some of the difficulties which may arise in meeting those objectives.

PROVIDING SERVICES FOR PEOPLE WITH AUTISM

Adults with autism are to be found in the widest possible range of settings – their own families, small supported group homes, medium sized hostels, core and cluster facilities, urban and rural specialist communities, mental handicap hospitals and institutions. The approach in each of these varies according to the social and political beliefs of the service-providers, the general outlook of the care providers, local attitudes, the type of organization making the provision, the functional level of the clients and, frequently, the amount of finance available. There will be a different emphasis from one setting to another – educational, custodial, interventionist, non-interventionist, conservative and innovative. This diversity serves to underline a remarkable inconsistency in the way some of the basic issues affecting people with autism are tackled.

Standardizing services

Although quality services are sometimes provided by a specific organization or establishment, this does not solve what is a general problem. There is a need systematically to develop effective solutions to the problems of providing care for adults with autism; there is also a need to disseminate those solutions for wider application. To take account of the range of ability, a range of provision will always be required but an attempt should be made to standardize the principles on which services are designed and delivered. This implies having a close look at the people who require help, identifying their needs and problems, and offering solutions which are likely to be of overall benefit. Since the component parts of the service may be varied in degree or type of structure, supervision, external support, or level of motivation, individualization can still occur.

Three major gains would be made from a standardized approach to service delivery design for adults who are autistic:

1. Care and education systems of known cost and effectiveness could be made available for general use;
2. Costly, local re-invention of effective strategies would be avoided;
3. Ineffective and inappropriate services would be minimized and scarce resources more profitably utilized.

Responding to need

Services which respond to the needs of people with autism can be grouped under two main headings: direct and indirect services.

Direct services

These include:

1. *Provision of food, shelter and care* in a range of residential options which appropriately serve the varying needs of people with autism. The spectrum of disability in the autistic group is very wide and services should accommodate this diversity.

2. *Provision of activities* which are focused on teaching people with autism the skills they need in order to increase their level of independence, degree of social integration, and ability to fulfil valued social roles. These activities should also promote the health, personal development and psychological well-being of people with autism through appropriate and adequate intervention in response to their needs.

3. *Provision of social, leisure and recreation activities* which offer frequent and varied opportunities for productive and enjoyable use of free time by people who are autistic. This will often exercise the ingenuity of carers because people with autism are inclined to use free time to withdraw.

4. *Use of individualized assessment, planning and instructional procedures* which respond to identified need in order to ensure that the potential of individual clients is recognized and enhanced.

Indirect services

These include:

1. *Information and evaluation systems* which gather, analyse and utilize data on individual clients, programmes and systems to establish objectives for services and policies; to assess the effectiveness of services and policies in meeting goals; and to modify programmes in line with the outcome of the evaluation. A highly specific approach is necessary since the person who is autistic can never be considered as other than unique.

2. *Personnel management practices* which recruit, train, deploy and retain adequate numbers of skilled practitioners and other workers to provide the services needed by people with autism. Working with people who are autistic is specialized and demanding: staff recruitment and support must reflect this reality.

3. *Promotion of public acceptance,* community involvement, professional commitment, and government and local authority policies which acknowledge the necessity for a specific response to the needs of people with autism. Often, it is a struggle to convince those in authority of the worthiness of the autistic cause. No opportunity should ever be wasted to demonstrate how proper provision can fundamentally improve the lives of people who are autistic.

4. *Development and sharing of knowledge and experience* among service providers, academic and research workers, public agencies, professional organizations and families.

5. *Promotion of the human rights and dignity* of people with autism in any setting.

Principles of service design

The general principles of direct service provision are very similar to those applied to other groups of people with a mental handicap. Appropriate services should be available to people who are autistic, regardless of the degree of handicap, and should recognize the dignity and value of the individual. Facilities should be tailored to meet individual needs rather than group or other requirements and the pattern of normal life should be reflected in terms of the working

Figure 6.1 Utilization of data collected on an individual basis.

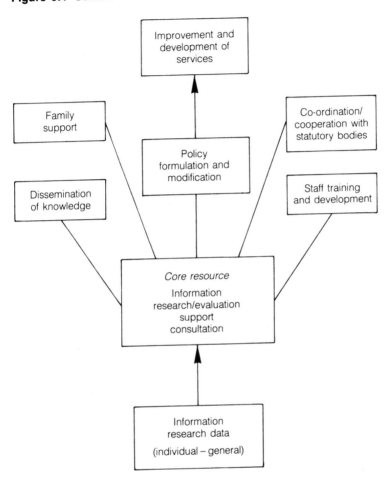

week, week-end activities and variations in daytime/evening routines. Full use should be made of community facilities and natural social networks.

So far as indirect services are concerned, the aim is to build in the support the individual requires in order to benefit from the typical facilities which exist for other members of the community. An essential principle of indirect service delivery is to collect information on an individual basis and to utilize this data in ways demonstrated by Figure 6.1.

Normalization

Any discussion about services for adolescents and adults with autism would be incomplete without some consideration of the principle of normalization. It is not proposed to examine the many issues arising out of the principle in detail but simply to restate it and to consider some of the difficulties which can arise when it is applied to services for people with autism.

Normalization has been described as 'the use of means which are valued in our society in order to develop and support personal behaviour, experiences and characteristics which are likewise valued'. It is concerned with what a service is trying to achieve and the means used to achieve it. In judging what a service provides, proponents of normalization ask 'how would an ordinary member of the community feel in the same circumstances?' The difficulties which arise in trying to apply the principle of normalization to services for people who are autistic can be grouped under three headings – general, organizational and client-related.

1. *General difficulties* – a major difficulty is inadequate understanding of 'normalization'. Many people take the idea to mean an attempt to make people who are autistic 'normal' whereas it is really about considering clients as people first with their handicap as an extra dimension. This lack of understanding is often accompanied by a negative social attitude which devalues people with any sort of handicap. Negative attitudes increase in relation to people with autism because of their inherent difficulties in initiating social interchanges.

A practical problem to arise is the inadequate allocation of resources to develop high quality services which would embrace the principle of normalization and provide the challenge of higher expectations, increase opportunities for personal development and enable people with autism to acquire more socially valued characteristics. The high staff to resident ratio in specialist establishments is often questioned but the job simply cannot be done unless there are opportunities for face-to-face instruction. This is only possible when the staff ratio is appropriate.

2. *Organizational difficulties* – frequently normalization is recognized as desirable by managers and staff but there is no real commitment to applying the principle to practice. Many sorts of excuses are advanced but often the prime reason is that putting

normalization into practice is difficult in any setting and there seems to be enough problems associated with people who are autistic without creating any more.

Sometimes, however, there is an affirmed commitment to the principle but it never becomes a reality because of lack of staff awareness or inadequate training – or because of adverse environmental factors such as physical isolation.

3. *Client difficulties* – the global problem here is in trying to 'reduce the differentness' of the person with autism (while simultaneously increasing the public's degree of acceptance of differentness). In many cases, people with autism have already been placed into specialist facilities which set them apart from other people. Whilst specialized provision can be adequately defended on several counts, it can compound the problem of social integration. Additionally, there are the factors influencing the capacity of people who are autistic to adapt to society. This ability depends on three main skills:

a) Being able to think and to use language;
b) Being able to handle interpersonal relationships effectively;
c) Being able to live independently in terms of self-care and vocational activities.

Clearly, many people with autism have problems with all of these and it is essential to try and teach them the complex skills which will allow them to fit more easily into society. The areas which present the greatest difficulties are:

1. Social interaction
2. Communication
3. Behaviours which are seen as 'strange' by others
4. Aggressive behaviour
5. Lack of initiative
6. Lack of ability to make choices and take decisions.

Age appropriateness

Closely related to the principle of normalization is the concept of age-appropriateness. For many people who are autistic, the normal human development pattern has been disrupted and, although they may mature physically, they perform intellectually, socially and emotionally in a childlike, sometimes inappropriate fashion. Consequently, there may be a tendency to treat older people with autism like children, placing them in a situation where they are rendered even more different from their peers than their handicap dictates. Areas in which age-appropriateness should be identified and applied are:

1. Language
2. Dress and grooming
3. Residential and work environments
4. Personal possessions
5. Leisure activities
6. Interaction opportunities.

Language

Adults should be addressed as such, normal words and tone of voice should be used without any hint of paternalism. Topics of interest can be found to develop conversation and the use of open-ended questions (starting with words like 'who', 'why', 'where', and 'how') will help ensure that the client gets the opportunity to speak for him or herself.

In the case of adults who use non-verbal language systems, it is important to give them enough time to express themselves adequately and not stifle their attempts by concluding the 'conversation' once the general drift of meaning has been obtained. The words of the song 'I just wondered . . . did you ever? . . . all the time . . .' illustrates the effect of this technique admirably.

Dress and grooming

Clothing and hairstyles should be typical of the person's age and there should be considerable effort to enable individual choices to be made. Clothing should also be in keeping with the occasion so that blouses and skirts, or jeans, may be alright for work but something more dressy can be encouraged for discos, nights out at the pub or visits to the theatre. Training for dress sense, including which colours go with which (and how to wear clothes properly rather than just put them on) should be part of any curriculum. How people present themselves can greatly influence how they are accepted. Designer stubbles are fine if contrived but, if they really only represent a lack of effort to shave properly, they can be a negative feature.

Residential and work environments

The environment within which we live and work has an effect on our general functioning and responses. For the adult who is autistic, the physical environment – whatever its purpose – should make age-appropriate demands for good judgement, adaptation and the development of more complex behaviour. Ideally, this means providing buildings to meet people's needs but this is often not possible. Where compromises have to be made, the main criterion should be that accommodation represents a standard and mode of living which would be acceptable to most people in the age range of the people for whom it is provided.

In terms of location, a school of thought exists which takes community integration to imply living right in the middle of a town – anything vaguely rural is unacceptable. The fact that many people choose to live in rural areas is conveniently forgotten. There are obviously extremes to be avoided and, if a general rule is required, it should take into account the necessity to offer the adult who is autistic the same social, recreational and vocational opportunities as anyone else of the same age.

Personal possessions

Most people have the right to acquire and keep personal possessions and this should also be the right of adults with autism. It may be necessary to guide some people away from choices which are clearly well below their chronological age and to reinforce the selection of appropriate items. There should be a degree of flexibility, however, particularly when people decide to spend their money on 'whims' such as snacks, refreshments and small gifts.

The suitability of possessions varies according to circumstances. It may be quite acceptable to have a large soft toy in your bedroom as part of the decor but to get on the bus to go shopping with it under your arm is a different matter. If the desire to lock away possessions – especially small items – is expressed, this should be respected and suitable facilities provided. Sometimes it is necessary to protect one person's property from another resident. The most unlikely items (bars of soap, toothbrushes) can be the target of an obsessional 'collector'.

Leisure activities

This major area will be the subject of later discussion but, in terms of age-appropriateness, it is essential to encourage the right balance between leisure, education, work and 'free time'. Fortunately, many recreational pursuits are common to all age groups and it is fairly easy to provide activities which meet individual needs and are, at the same time, age-typical.

Opportunities for interaction

Given the socializing deficits of people with autism, interaction opportunities are of major importance. Adults should be encouraged to be active participants in a variety of individual and group relationships in a range of community settings. It is particularly helpful if they can be involved in activities with age-peers, especially people who are really interested in them. Sometimes it is possible to link a person who is autistic with someone who has a common interest, and this can be socially productive. Local clubs, societies, organizations and churches usually respond very positively if they have an opportunity to discover what people with autism are like. A substantial degree of support may be necessary in introducing people with autism into unaccustomed social settings but this can be gradually withdrawn as new relationships develop. Learning how to cope socially can only be learnt in society, therefore no opportunity should ever be lost to permit the man or woman who is autistic to use and develop such socializing skills as he or she may have developed.

CARING FOR ADULTS WHO ARE AUTISTIC

Most people who have reached adulthood use their previous experience, knowledge, training, relationships, successes and failures to map out a route for their future lives. This may involve decisions about how a career should be pursued, what will give job satisfaction, how leisure time should be used, how money should be spent, how to make best use of the intellect, and so on. It would be a strange person indeed who did not engage in some sort of self-assessment and planning for at least a few years ahead.

The majority of people with autism have not managed to acquire many of the skills which other people take for granted. They are also unable to plan for their own future either in terms of long-term or short-term development. The responsibility for such planning mostly devolves to someone else; often the way in which the plan is constructed and followed will dictate both the pace and extent of development of the person who is autistic.

During school years, the plan is generally clearly prescribed and the requirement to follow it obligatory but, in adulthood, there is often a resistance by carers to adopt the same procedure, either because they see it as an intrusion on personal liberty or because it is considered inappropriate or superfluous. It is widely recognized, however, that good care in any setting depends on an adequate assessment of need and the application of a planned programme to meet that need, both assessment and programme being regularly reviewed and amended in the light of experience.

The needs of adults with autism

Adults who are autistic have needs which fall into five main categories:

1. Physical health
2. Safety, security, structure
3. Relationships, love
4. Confidence, self-esteem
5. Self-fulfilment, autonomy.

These are needs which are common to all humanity: the main difference lies in ease of attainment. The person who is autistic may require only a little help in some areas and a very large amount of assistance in others. Successful 'carers' will be able to identify what the needs of the person with autism are, plan to provide the necessary help and resources to meet them, put the plan into action, and check whether it is succeeding or not. This should not be a haphazard process but should instead be a carefully considered and conscientiously applied procedure.

Caring – a client-centred process model

The main components of the caring process – assessment, planning, implementation and evaluation – can be shown in diagrammatic form

Figure 6.2 The main components of the caring process.

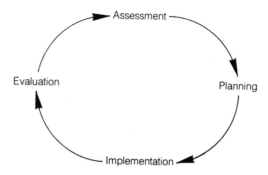

(Figure 6.2). Figure 6.2 clearly demonstrates the cyclical nature of the process which is continuous and which requires regular up-dating.

PROVIDING CONTINUING CARE, TRAINING AND EDUCATION FOR THE ADULT WHO IS AUTISTIC

Training for life skills

To function adequately within community settings of varying complexity, people with autism must possess a wide range of skills. These range from basic self-care to fairly complex interactions with many different people in diverse social, occupational and recreational environments. Instructional programmes for adolescent and adult people with autism typically include:

1. Daily living skills
2. Numeracy and literacy skills
3. Socializing skills
4. Vocational training and preparation
5. Recreational skills

In each of these areas, there is a direct relationship to real life situations and the whole could be described as a functional (as opposed to an academic) curriculum. A functional curriculum requires functional assessment as a foundation for planning, monitoring and evaluating instruction. Information is assembled with the aim of providing a profile of the person's relative strengths and weaknesses. The purpose of the assessment is really to provide the basis of a working plan on which instruction can be built. It is the first part of a process, consisting of four steps:

1. Completing the assessment;
2. Determining learning objectives and deciding the teaching strategy which will accomplish them;
3. Carrying out the teaching;
4. Checking whether learning has taken place.

Assessment

Assessment is about collecting and studying information about a person then using it to assist his or her development. The information can be collected by two methods. The first method is direct observation; the second method is interview. Observation requires close attention to the person and the activities he or she is engaged in. To get a clear picture, this may involve sustained observation in different settings over a period of several days. Interviews are conducted with the individual or, more usually in the case of people who are autistic, with someone who knows him or her well. A list of questions is used, sometimes of a general nature and sometimes relating to a specific skills area. The questions should be framed in language which is easily understood. In professional care settings, it is common for these questions to be addressed to the teams of people responsible for the client (keyworker, instructor, and so on) and a composite picture of the person's abilities obtained.

Goals and learning objectives

Assessment tells us where we are at a particular point in time but we have to have something to progress towards. In planning instruction for people who are autistic, it is important to set the long-term and short-term priorities which will define the direction of individual progress. Goals may cover a period of six months or a year and should state what the overall expectations are for the person at the end of that time.

Behavioural objectives, like goals, are written statements which define the progress the person is expected to make. Objectives are really the steps which are necessary to reach the goal. There are three fundamental elements to a behavioural objective:

1. The behaviour to be learned;
2. The conditions under which the behaviour will occur;
3. How well or to what criterion the behaviour must be performed.

The first element says what the person will be able to do. For instance, Fred will put on his shirt. The second component states the conditions under which the behaviour will occur. For instance, Fred will button his shirt having been given a verbal prompt; or, Fred will button his shirt without assistance. The third element says how well or to what criterion the behaviour must be performed. This is critical because it defines when the person has accomplished the objective.

The criteria applied will vary greatly but will include statements about accuracy, speed, duration or quantity of behaviour. It is worth repeating that behavioural objectives are statements of what the person will learn not what or how it will be taught.

Goals and objectives are not much use unless they are written down. Often they are incorporated into a personal plan to which people can refer.

Individual programme plans

The Individual Programme Plan (IPP) is a widely used tool for making decisions about present needs and for developing resources to increase an individual's positive characteristics and capacity for independence. It can be used in both home and work settings and should include:

1. A statement of the current level of performance;
2. A statement of long-term goals and short/medium term objectives (which have already been mentioned);
3. Criteria which identify the standards and conditions under which the objectives will be considered to have been achieved;
4. A list of special resources which are likely to be required;
5. The date on which performance will be re-assessed.

IPPs should not be paper exercises. Used properly, they are a means of ensuring that individual strengths are developed in a systematic and dynamic way.

Instruction – problems of generalization and maintenance

With patience, perseverance and the right approach, people who are autistic can be helped to acquire many new skills. A major problem, however, is that they may only be able to use these skills under very specific conditions and not manage to carry them over into different environments or use them appropriately. For example, someone may learn to push the vacuum cleaner back and forth to clean the carpet but not appreciate that it has to be moved to different areas of the room to do the job properly.

The application of a skill in appropriate circumstances is called 'generalization' and this can be very difficult to convey to people with autism. 'Maintenance' is the term used to describe the continuing use of a skill after instruction and reinforcement (or prompting) have ceased. Again, getting people who are autistic to maintain relatively simple tasks, such as face-washing, can be an extremely challenging task.

The literature of special education is full of successful examples of teaching strategies, designed to promote skill acquisition. However, within the same literature, there is a distinct scarcity of any system which ensures the performance of these skills both outside the training setting and over a period of time (i.e. generalization and maintenance). If the aim of education and training is to prepare people to cope in more complex and demanding environments, it is important to provide some means of ensuring that they carry the skills with them into new settings. The 'train and hope' method has been identified in the literature: this means that the target behaviours are trained and the occurrence of generalized effects are sometimes assessed but not specifically planned. Unfortunately there do not appear to be any comprehensive strategies which promote generalization and maintenance but there are several methods which do offer some promise.

Functional skills training

In the context of generalization and maintenance, training skills which are functional (useful in a practical sense) increases the likelihood that the individual will use them to obtain reinforcement which will in turn help to perpetuate the skill.

Training for the same skill in a variety of environments

'Classroom teaching' in workshops or homes provides instructors or care workers with the opportunity to present rules and examples clearly and to provide clients with practice opportunities and constructive feed-back in a non-threatening environment. To ensure generalization of skills learned in formal surroundings, the individual must eventually be exposed to the stimuli, variations and consequences of community, or other appropriate, settings and be encouraged to practice the skill in these settings.

Self-control

Self-control has been defined as people 'directing, maintaining and co-ordinating their actions without continuous supervision'. Obviously this has major implications for the generalization and maintenance of skills and, although the area still has to be fully researched (particularly in regard to the actual skills required for self-control), it does look very promising. One method is to use a simple recording system in which the person notes whether he or she has done (or not done) the necessary task. This self-monitoring device can also be used to check performance, for example, whether the person got dressed quickly or slowly in the morning.

Long-term monitoring

A variety of circumstances can conspire to ensure that skills deteriorate. Changes in environmental factors, diminished opportunity or requirement to use skills, lack of reinforcement, are some. It is, therefore, necessary to provide gradually decreasing checks for continuing performance and to make the adjustments which changes in settings and situations dictate. It may also be necessary to provide some 'top-up' training from time to time.

EDUCATION, LEISURE AND WORK OPPORTUNITIES FOR PEOPLE WITH AUTISM

Educational opportunities

It is widely maintained that the most effective response to the needs of people with autism is an educational one. For the adult who is autistic, it should offer, not only the skills training component previously described, but the widest possible range of experiences in a similarly wide range of settings. The list of possibilities is endless and it is important never to underestimate the capacity of people with autism to learn and enjoy new experiences. In any case, like the rest of us, people who are autistic can only communicate about what they feel or what they know. Without new experiences, their potential for communication can be severely limited.

Leisure and recreation provision

Participation in leisure and recreation activities has become an important aspect of life in our society. These activities promote physical health, provide opportunities to develop social relationships and can promote positive self-concepts and confidence. Using community-based recreation and leisure facilities provides a natural setting to build competence and improve social interactions for people who are autistic.

It is important to clarify what leisure actually is. Leisure is time not spent in work or other required tasks (such as domestic, self-care or vocational activities). During leisure, activities should be based on individual choice. In the past, leisure has been equated with free time or with time not spent on specified activities. It is easy to understand a reluctance to support increased free time for people who are autistic because of the inordinate amount of time they can spend in passive, aimless activity. Indeed, a major criticism of institutional care is the lack of meaningful activity for clients and the excessive periods of 'down time' when people are left to their own devices. Some researchers have also observed a higher incidence of negative behaviours (e.g. rocking and head-banging) during free time. The critical factor, however, is how free time is used, not the amount which is available.

Personal preferences

For a person to make meaningful choices and exercise preferences, two requirements must be satisfied:

1. A reasonable range of leisure activity is available;
2. The person has the necessary skills to make and communicate preferences.

The second of these raises questions about the acquisition of leisure/recreation skills and it would appear that traditional education has emphasized intellectual, vocational and daily living skills to the neglect of skills required for leisure and recreation. This seems all the more unfortunate when it has been demonstrated that, because

139

participation with others is an inherent part of many of these activities, social interaction skills can be improved through leisure pursuits.

Leisure and recreation skills training

For the most part, people who are autistic lack the ability spontaneously to choose a leisure activity. It is beneficial to provide them with the opportunity to acquire a variety of leisure skills and then help them to decide which ones they prefer. As with work, leisure activities can create a feeling of fulfilment and confidence and can contribute to personal growth. The first stage of developing leisure activities is to look at the individual and identify:

1. Other areas in which he or she has shown interest;
2. His or her ability to co-ordinate movements;
3. The extent of his or her ability to interact;
4. The level of his or her understanding.

Once this assessment has been completed, it is then important to consider a variety of activities, the requirements of which match individual preferences and strengths: there is no point in suggesting a game, the rules of which are so complex they would never be understood. It is also futile to proceed unless the person seems happy with the proposed activity. Enjoyment should be a major consideration in reaching an eventual decision.

Systematic instruction is necessary to provide the skills both to carry out the selected activity and to encourage participation. The patterns of learning and methods of teaching are basically the same as in other areas of daily living skills and will not be elaborated. There are, however, a few special considerations which are worth examining.

Normalization and leisure activities

The opportunity should be provided for men and women with autism to engage in age-appropriate activities, at appropriate times, in suitable settings. Not all the activities need be community-based by any means but, where this is the case, the aim should be to integrate one or two people into those sports or facilities where their presence will not only be tolerated but actively encouraged. Emphasis should be placed on social acceptability and enjoyment by the client. If these are not in evidence, the approach has to be modified. Frequently, it is necessary to provide staff support to ensure that integration proceeds unhindered. This underlines the necessity for a high staff ratio in all spheres of activity.

Range of leisure activities

Many people are inclined to stress the activity aspect of leisure and interpret this as requiring vigorous muscular exercise of one sort or another. This can be beneficial but is by no means essential. Some people who are autistic may enjoy swimming, table tennis or hill walking but others will be perfectly happy cooking, going out for a meal, to the cinema or concert, or doing a jigsaw puzzle. The best leisure programmes are those which offer a wide variety of pursuits and slot individual people into them as required. It is also worth remembering that what is work to one person can be play to another. One man's favourite pastime is brushing the yard which most of us would consider a boring task.

Vacations for adults with autism

As a subject this has received scant consideration, if any, in the literature of autism. This is quite remarkable when one considers the way most people anticipate their annual holiday, plan it, spend money on it and, hopefully, enjoy it. Holidays can be as beneficial for people who are autistic as for any one else. They break the routine of life and offer a change of location, food, scenery, people, activities. Certainly there has to be much thought given to the number of people who go on holiday together and who accompanies them. Depending on the people involved, accommodation can vary from special holiday facilities in rugged areas to university flats, commercial premises or mobile homes in ordinary holiday towns. For people living in residential homes, the problem is often one of staffing but this can be partially remedied by using a mix of instructional and residential staff with perhaps a volunteer or two.

The duration of a holiday can be critical. In some circumstances a week or more would not present a problem but, with some client groups, a few days of suitable activity is more appropriate.

The important principles to observe are tailoring the location, accommodation, staff support and activities to the needs of the individuals and making every effort to ensure that the experience is an enjoyable one.

141

Providing work for adults with autism

There is a theory that an occupation only becomes satisfying when the individual is able to derive from it a sense of personal growth. This implies the person feels he or she is developing in wisdom and experience, becoming more independent and competent, and having the opportunity to exercise and expand whatever potential he or she has. This has considerable significance for the person who is autistic: self-esteem and confidence gained through work are almost as important as proper nutrition and regular exercise.

The provision of vocational training and work opportunities is fraught with many difficulties. There is a choice between supplying some form of work-based therapeutic activity in a sheltered environment, or of providing useful work opportunities in a disciplined setting (having developed a specific skill which contributes to a viable business enterprise or which can be transferred to a competitive job situation). In the prevailing economic climate, it seems unlikely that people who are autistic will be absorbed as part of any sort of work force. In any event, only a few people with autism are likely to succeed in a competitive work situation because of their inability to adapt to change, or because of their obsessive and socially inappropriate behaviours (or because of the negative social attitude of others).

Nevertheless, there is a requirement to provide some sort of 'work', the essential components of which must be that it has an identifiable and useful end product, or provides a service, and that it has some intrinsic benefit for the individual. If the product is marketable and the person concerned is aware of this and can benefit, even indirectly, so much the better.

There are some ground rules to be observed in the provision of work opportunities for people with autism.

Practical considerations

Wherever possible, working environments should be at some distance from the residential base so that there is a sense of 'going out to work'. Using ordinary industrial or commercial premises reduces the feeling of segregation and is more reality-based.

Staff should be trained in teaching/training methods and should make full use of appropriate psychological and behavioural methods to develop abilities and skills; they should be given regular opportunities to investigate and suggest new materials as well as new methods for incorporation in revised skills programmes. There should be continual evaluation of the effectiveness of the work programme so that responses to needs can be up-dated.

Resources should be provided which permit a variety of skills to be acquired and used: this avoids monotony for both clients and staff. Every client should have an individual programme of work which is regularly reviewed and client preferences should be taken into account in creating work programmes. A high level of supervision and support will ensure that clients cope with the work and do not become frustrated; this will also enable the work to achieve a reasonably high commercial standard, although the temptation for staff to do too much must be avoided. The end product should mainly be the work of the client, not of staff.

Safety aspects

The increasing emphasis on meaningful work means that more people who are autistic are exposed to power tools and machinery. Many have no sense of danger and must therefore be trained in the safe use of this equipment. The risk of accidents can be reduced by basic safety practices – working in clean, well-lit areas, using guards and clamps to hold work in place, wearing safety glasses, face masks and proper industrial clothing, ensuring that electrical machinery is connected via a residual current circuit breaker, and having regular equipment checks and safety audits by an independent expert. Chemicals and other agents should be stored only in the correct containers – never in anything which resembles a food container or refreshment bottle. Dangerous chemicals should be stored in locked cupboards and only the amount required for the job withdrawn.

Handling of materials

To avoid back injury, clients should be taught how to lift properly and the use of proper work gloves will reduce the risk of cuts, wood splinters and other hand injuries. Vocational training centres and workshops should have accident prevention programmes for both staff and clients. This does not mean over-protection. If people are prepared properly, they can cope with complex working environments. Despite preventative measures, accidents can still happen. Staff should be adequately trained in first aid so that, should an emergency in the workshop occur, prompt and effective action can be taken.

Work space

People who are autistic appear to work best in small groups which can be easily supervised. Where two or more groups share a common working area, this must be large enough to enable each group to function quite independently of the other.

ADULTS WITH 'PROBLEM' BEHAVIOUR

Having provided the best possible residential and workshop facilities and staffed them with sufficient, well-trained, supported and motivated members of staff, it might be reasonable to expect that all should run smoothly. However, in the best organized households, there is always the possibility of someone doing something which is not acceptable and if this happens regularly we have to consider how to tackle the problem.

The concept of normalization implies not only the development of 'normal' environments, like the ordinary household, but also the acquisition by the person with a handicap of the skill/knowledge repertoires needed to interact appropriately with that environment and with the people in it. Consequently, if people with autism are to function successfully in society, it is essential to isolate the variables which interfere with their ability to function in a normal environment. And behaviour problems have been identified as major impediments to successful community living and adjustment.

Assessment of problem behaviour

There is a need to find more accurate methods of predicting the adaptation to the community of people who are autistic. If behaviour problems are a major source of community rejection, it should at least be possible to identify more exactly the problems which are responsible. This may mean being more specific – avoiding vague terms such as 'hyperactivity', 'disruptive', 'self-stimulating', 'challenging behaviours', 'aggressive tendencies'. Being specific would go some way towards understanding and remedying precise problem behaviours.

When considering problem behaviours, negative assessment (that is observing a person who is autistic in terms of deficits rather than assets) can be detrimental. Certainly, emphasis on negative attributes is undesirable. Individual actions become a problem when they adversely affect the individual, the physical environment, or others. The types of behaviour which seem to persist into adulthood in people with autism can be grouped under three headings.

Maladaptive behaviours

These are socially unpleasant to other people, interfere with the individual's capacity to cope with environmental demands, or are repetitious or bizarre. They include flapping arms, failing to follow instructions with great obstinacy, and pacing.

Disruptive behaviours

These are the behaviours which demand inappropriate attention from others and negatively affect the environment. Screaming, stamping of feet, running around wildly come into this category.

Destructive behaviours

This group embraces behaviours which pose a threat to the individual, to those around, or to property. They require an immediate response to prevent injury. Examples are hitting others, throwing objects, biting others, head-banging.

There are several points about problem behaviours to be borne in mind when considering strategies for changing them. Often behaviour problems would be regarded as inconsequential if they were performed by people without handicaps. Some football fans and people leaving pubs are a good example of this.

Although problem behaviours can be bothersome or socially unacceptable, only about 16% are considered to jeopardize the health, safety or general welfare of other people. Responses to problem behaviours are frequently influenced by the attitudes and personal experience (or lack of it) of the individuals being subjected to the behavioural excess. In other words, people do get used to idiosyncratic behaviour. The way people respond to a particular problem behaviour may be related to how they perceive their own ability to cope with it, or else to previous adverse experiences in a similar situation.

There may be a lack of agreement as to what constitutes serious problem behaviour. Often this depends on the frame of reference in which the behaviour is viewed. If it is accepted that a major goal for people who are autistic is the achievement of a life-style which is as independent as possible, it is important to concentrate on the reduction or eradication of behaviours which:

1. Are most likely to have negative social consequences for the individual;
2. Are most likely to have a negative effect on other people;
3. Are most likely to prevent other people from initiating and maintaining social interaction with the person who is autistic.

Strategies for managing behaviour

There are many different ways of approaching the management of 'difficult' or 'problem' behaviours and no attempt will be made to deal with these at any length. However, it may be useful to outline some general principles, bearing in mind that the selection of strategies for managing behaviour must be consistent both with the overall development goals for the individual person with autism and with the concept of normalization. This implies that behaviour management strategies should:

1. Be as non-aversive as possible;
2. Facilitate the development of adaptive social skills;
3. Be both efficient and effective.

Punishment strategies

These have been notoriously ineffective in bringing about significant changes in behaviour. In addition to their lack of usefulness, they often lead to further undesirable behaviours – running away, aggression, emotional distress.

Adaptive social development

In simple terms, this means the reduction of problem behaviours by developmental skill training (without any other sort of intervention). An example of this is the prompting and reinforcement of social interaction, resulting in increased social responsibilities and a reduction in 'withdrawn' behaviour – engage people in conversation and they will not sit and stare out of the window.

Positive reinforcement

This can be used to strengthen the positive behaviours mentioned in the preceding paragraph. There are many texts which deal with the subject of reinforcement in detail. In this context, the points worth remembering are:

1. Reinforcers should be easy and convenient to provide;
2. Reinforcers should not disrupt established routines;
3. Reinforcers should be varied for the same situation;
4. Reinforcers should be consistent with the principle of normalization.

Environmental factors

Potentially aversive environmental factors which may contribute to problem behaviours are noise, proximity to others, odours, unstimulating routines, pain (undiagnosed toothache, for example), absence of attention, negative reactions from other people, physical discomfort (too cold, too warm, hunger, thirst). Creating the right environment may not provide the whole answer but it often sets the scene for an improved response to other techniques.

Self-determination

This does not mean letting people have their own way all the time. What it does mean is developing environments which include decision-making and which provide opportunities for acquired, positive responses to occur. Examples include:

1. Deciding what to wear;
2. Selecting leisure activities;
3. Choosing food at mealtimes.

This enhances decision-making processes which can ultimately be used to enable the client to decide not to indulge in a problem behaviour (self-control) which is infinitely preferable to other techniques.

Management through drugs

This is included because any mention of behavioural management strategies would be incomplete without a reference to it. Most people prefer to use other methods but there are occasions when psychotropic drugs can be a useful adjunct to other strategies. Unfortunately, the use of drugs on their own as a method of controlling behaviour is often excessive and abused. In addition, many drug treatment programmes for reducing problem behaviour have a habit of going on forever, without any proper evaluation of whether they are producing any positive effect.

STRESS AND BURNOUT IN WORKING WITH PEOPLE WHO ARE AUTISTIC

So far we have been considering the best ways of responding to the needs of the adult who is autistic but these responses can only be made if 'carers' are willing and able to take on the task. Mostly this proceeds smoothly but, now and again, the miracle workers who remain calm at all times, know all the answers, find the work rewarding, love all those they serve and so on, suddenly find they have hit a significant bump in the road.

The subject of stress and burnout is common to both the families of people with autism and people in the caring professions (teachers, instructors, houseparents, care officers, social workers). Job-related stress and burnout in autistic services differ from the stress and tedium which tend to afflict people in industry and commerce. The differences are due to the type of need and the nature of the work involved in responding to that need.

The terms stress and burnout are sometimes used synonymously but they actually refer to two different phenomena. Most people in a caring situation experience stress. Stress can be controlled, but uncontrolled stress leads to burnout. Stress is defined as a response of the human body to demands placed upon it and its impact is determined by how each individual reacts to and interprets the stressful situation. People constantly adjust and readjust to positive and negative stresses. Burnout occurs when, as a result of continuing intense and negative pressures, a person finds no meaning or attraction in his or her job. It can result from the constant emotional pressure and stress of working intensely and over a long period of time with people who are autistic. There are generally three signs of burnout:

Low energy levels

People who have reached burnout feel constantly tired.

Emotional exhaustion

People feel sorry for themselves and provide little or no support to others.

Mental exhaustion

People develop negative attitudes towards themselves, their jobs and even those who care for them. They often feel depressed and worthless. Most people enter the caring professions to help others. In burnout, the initial attitude of compassion turns to not caring. The desire to help and to make a contribution, and the urge to work creatively, turn into a 'nobody really cares' mentality.

A common symptom is undirected anger. This is anger not justified by specific circumstances: it boils and ferments near the surface. Unfulfilled expectations of one sort or another fuel the anger, then it is directed against colleagues, superiors or even clients.

Causes of stress and burnout

One cause can be frustrated role expectations. A major problem here is role ambiguity, particularly true for staff in small group settings. Staff members may be unsure whether they are a substitute parent, teacher, counsellor, residential social worker, or what. Each of these titles implies a slightly different role. Staff working with people who are autistic need very clear role definitions. Without this, stress is almost inevitable.

Another cause is work overload. There are two potential problems – working excessive hours or trying to squeeze too much work into regular hours. The end result is often the same – a lowering of standards in the work performed with a consequent deterioration in the development of the people being cared for.

Another cause is the demands of care work. By definition, caring services respond to people who have a need. This creates reactive situations in which staff members must continually confront, and endeavour to respond to, people's needs and problems. The irony is that when you are successful and meet these needs, clients tend to move on to something different, their places filled by others with needs.

Many staff members have difficulty leaving work issues at work. Indeed, for live-in residential staff, this is virtually impossible. This leads to two complications:

1. Staff cannot find relief from the needs and demands of others;
2. Staff inject work stress into their own home life.

Staff in services for people with autism also feel stress when they are given very limited authority. They are asked to assist people in developing new skills and making decisions but, at the same time, they perhaps play no part in the unit's planning processes.

Finally, working with people who are autistic is acknowledged to have a big potential for frustration and stress. The teaching of new skills and behaviours can be repetitive and time-consuming. In some cases, clients show negative behaviours, such as aggression, which are often not predicted. Much of the time, the staff member is putting a great deal of effort into trying to sustain interaction and getting very little in return.

Controlling stress

The first step is to understand what is causing the stress – is it work-induced, self-created or produced by a particular client? Sometimes there is a combination of factors and it is useful if these can be isolated from each other as they may require different sorts of responses.

A crucial strategy in reducing stress and avoiding burnout is the development of a social support network of people who share your ideas and values. They can provide help when it is needed in the following ways:

Listening

Someone who will just listen without giving advice or telling you how he or she had the same problem.

'Technical' support

Someone who will give you honest feedback on the work you do.

Emotional support

Someone to stick by you through challenging circumstances.

The techniques of coping with stress are many and varied and each person must find the approach which suits their needs best. There would seem to be eight different strategies which many systems have in common.

Exercise

To help relaxation and improve self-image. It is important to choose a form of exercise which can be undertaken easily and regularly and which is enjoyable.

Nutrition

Proper eating habits and good nutritional balance. The aim should be to eat to keep fit, avoiding excessive weight gain.

Opportunities for learning

Take a course on some subject unrelated to work. This can enrich your life, widen your horizons and help relaxation.

Setting sensible standards

Avoiding the self-destructive urge to compete with others. Aim at doing a good job for its own sake.

Variety

Preventing boredom in work and other situations: trying some new activity at work and outside of it.

Realism

Recognize what you can change and what is clearly not within your power to change. Accept the limits you have identified.

Pace yourself

High gear may be acceptable for some of the time but it cannot be kept up for ever.

Positively plan for relaxation

Try to avoid working outside of working hours or taking work problems home. Although discussing problems with a friend, relative or partner can sometimes provide an important outlet, it can also recreate the stressful experience.

People who work with children and adults with autism spend much of their time meeting the needs of others and often forget about taking care of themselves. This may work for a time but in the long run we have to admit to not being superhuman and be prepared to ease the pressures on ourselves. That way the working of miracles can go on longer and more effectively.

FURTHER READING

Clements, J. (1987) *Severe Learning Disability and Psychological Handicap*, John Wiley & Sons, Chichester.
Fontana, D. (1989) *Managing Stress*, D.P.S. Routledge, London.
Halpern, A.S. and Fuhrer, M.J. (1984) *Functional Assessment in Rehabilitation*, Paul H. Brookes, Baltimore.
Lakin, K.C. and Bruininks, R.H. (1984) *Strategies for Achieving Community Integration of Developmentally Disabled Citizens*, Paul H. Brookes, Baltimore.
O'Brien, J. and Tyne, A. (1981) *The principle of normalization, a foundation for effective services*, C.M.H.E.R.A., London.
Schopler, E. and Mesibov, G.B. (1983) *Autism in Adolescents and Adults*, Plenum Press, New York.
Wolfensberger, W. (1972) *Normalisation*, N.I.M.R., Toronto.

Index